Anonymous

My Bible Class

with an essay on Bible-class teaching

Anonymous

My Bible Class
with an essay on Bible-class teaching

ISBN/EAN: 9783337100322

Printed in Europe, USA, Canada, Australia, Japan

Cover: Foto ©Lupo / pixelio.de

More available books at **www.hansebooks.com**

MY BIBLE CLASS:

WITH AN ESSAY ON

BIBLE-CLASS TEACHING.

BY
A SCRIPTURE TEACHER.

———◆———

PHILADELPHIA:
PERKINPINE & HIGGINS,
No. 56 N. Fourth Street.

CONTENTS.

PART I.

An Essay on Bible-Class Teaching.

	PAGE
I. Qualifications	7
II. His Aim	15
III. His Method	22

PART II.

My Bible Class, or Conversations on our Lord's Appearances to his Disciples after his Resurrection.

I. First Sabbath	40
II. Second Sabbath	52
III. Third Sabbath	64
IV. Fourth Sabbath	77
V. Fifth Sabbath	89

CONTENTS.

VI. Sixth Sabbath 103
VII. Seventh Sabbath 121
VIII. Eighth Sabbath 135
IX. Ninth Sabbath 148
X. Tenth Sabbath 163

BIBLE-CLASS TEACHING.

EVERY class in a well-conducted Sabbath-school will be a Scripture class. The lessons of the elementary reading-book and sentences of the letter-box will be but extracts from the word of God. Even the teacher of infants will earnestly endeavor to create an intelligent, and, as far as possible, a connected and progressive acquaintance with Bible truth. To the knowledge of Scripture every other kind of instruction will be helpful. The lesson in reading, the rehearsal of the catechism, the repetition of hymns will only be varied means of ensuring the one great result. The whole subject of Sunday-school instruction is therefore included under the title prefixed to these remarks. It is my intention, however, to refer chiefly to one department of this field of labor. In almost all schools now there are young people who have passed through the earlier grades of scriptural instruction, who are well versed in the principles of the doctrine of Christ, and whom no deficiency of merely secular knowledge any longer prevents from advancing to explore the revelation of God in its fullness and to comprehend it in its harmony. Such scholars, more than any others, need the guidance and control of wise, earnest and well-instructed minds. It is, then, to teachers in these higher sections of the school that the following hints are specially addressed. Let it, however, be borne in mind that the same general principles are applicable in the instruction of every grade. The lowest prepares for the highest, and in some degree commences its work. An efficient infant class is the best guarantee for a large and intelligent Bible class.

I do not profess to discuss the whole subject of senior classes. My business is not with their organization or discipline, but simply with their teaching. Nor would I attempt to exhaust even this topic. The limits to an article like the present forbid me to do more than state some general principles, and often a few practical hints; leaving their development and illustration to the conversations that follow.

The QUALIFICATIONS, the AIM and the METHOD of the Bible teacher are the three great things to be considered by all who would understand or attempt the work.

I.

QUALIFICATIONS.

It seems superfluous to say that teachers should be "mighty in the Scriptures." And yet a few words of explanation and of caution may not even here be out of place.

An acquaintance with Scripture is something far beyond a mere *familiarity with texts.* Perhaps the habit, now so prevalent in the pulpit, of discoursing successively from isolated and unconnected passages may have tended to create in the minds of Christians generally a very partial, fragmentary idea of Bible truth. At any rate, almost every Christian church, nay, every company of Sunday-school teachers, will afford abundant evidence that a familiar acquaintance with separate portions of the divine word may consist with an utter inability to comprehend it as a complete and harmonious whole. There are thousands of Bible-class teachers who never read the Bible consecutively themselves, much less with their scholars. They revert continually to favorite passages, with little regard even to the immediate connection in which they stand, or in dwelling upon a particular book, they give scarcely a thought to the place in the grand universal scheme which it occupies. The connection and mutual dependence of the divine dispensations is a subject upon which they have never reflected, nor have they ever known the interest and delight of tracing the successive stages in the development of spiritual truth, each more glorious than the last, until the whole were crowned by the gospel of the Son of God. It is evident that frequent mistake, and partial knowledge at the best, must be the result of such desultory study. These teachers may be familiar with many Scripture truths, but they cannot be said to know the Scriptures. They may exhort successfully, but they cannot expound intelligently. Their instructions will be an endless circle rather than a progressive course. And with all their honest and devoted attempts to do good, there will yet remain many a "height and depth" of sacred truth hidden alike from themselves and from those whom they attempt to teach.

Most strongly, therefore, would I urge the study of the Scripture *as a whole.* Let the entire Bible be read chronologically, and each book be studied consecutively. The present arrangement of the Bible is most injurious. It is true that the evils of the chapter and verse division are obviated by the "Paragraph Bible," a copy of which every teacher ought to possess. One step more is required to complete the benefit; that is, the publication of the Scriptures arranged, as far as possible, *in the order in which they were written.* In the mean time, it will be easy for every teacher, with a little pains and the aid of a table of chronology, to make the arrangement for himself.

It must be added that a consecutive acquaintance with the Bible is a very different thing from a familiarity with *systematic theology.* There are indeed advantages in the latter which are by no means to be depreciated. Yet it cannot be denied that theological knowledge often does exist together with a very considerable ignorance of the true extent and harmony of Scripture truth. Nay, such ignorance will be the very result of making theology the exclusive or the primary object of pursuit. A student, for instance, may have mastered the catechism with all its scriptural proofs, and yet not really know the Bible. It is impossible to mechanize the infinite truth of God into the compass of a human system. The attempt, moreover, is always dangerous. The relative position which the varied truths of Scripture sustain toward each other is almost sure to be disturbed. A disproportionate stress will be laid upon one passage, while another as truly important will be assigned an inferior place or abandoned to total neglect. The safest plan is to receive and study truth in the order in which God has given it. His teachings surely need not be rearranged by human skill before they can be comprehended. True, there is none of the form of system in the Bible, but there is the reality. Let a man but study the word of God consecutively, candidly, thoughtfully, and there will be little fear but a complete and harmonious image of Divine truth will be found in his mind. He may decompose that image afterward, if he please, and arrange its elements into a creed. This, however, must be the last step in his studies, not the first; the result, and not the guide of his investigations. The Scriptures, in a word, must be taken not to interpret, but to suggest, his creed.

The student will, of course, make diligent use of all accessible stores of information tending to cast illustrative light upon the sacred page. These are now most manifold. What with commentaries, biblical dictionaries and volumes of Scripture illustrations, perhaps there is greater danger of the teacher's acquiring a vast but undigested mass of knowledge than of his being left in helpless ignorance. Let him remember it is of more importance that his information should be well assorted than that it should be large. Let each item, therefore, be put at once into its proper place. In such matters an orderly arrangement is preferable even to a good memory; and although the teacher may not be able to carry the contents of libraries in his head, a great point is gained if he only knows where and how to look for each particular that he needs.

In studying with a more immediate view to the labors of the Sabbath, classes for mutual instruction will be very helpful. "Let the superintendent or minister, with the twenty or thirty teachers around him, give different members of the class distinct departments of inquiry; let one have biographical matter; let another come informed on matters of geography; a third on general history; a fourth on Jewish rites and customs; a fifth on Jewish history; and others on other topics. Let every teacher who attends in such a class do his part toward making his class useful both to himself and to others. Never avoid a question which an intelligent child may be expected to ask, and never be satisfied till the question is answered. The president will have little more to do than to suggest and guide the inquiries and replies. The class will be one of mutual instruction, and will have vast advantages over one in which the things to be said to the children are given to the teachers in the very words themselves that are to be employed."

Teachers who engage in such classes must recollect that the object is to inform their own minds, rather than to prepare the instruction to be given to the scholars. The latter object cannot be attained in any efficient manner by such association, inasmuch as each grade in the school will require a different style of presenting truth. A teacher once remarked to me, "I feel that this class is very useful to my own mind, but I want something for my children." She had forgotten that in her own improvement she was making the best preparation to instruct and benefit them. The teacher who understands a subject most thoroughly will be able to impart it most simply. It is a mistake to suppose that knowledge is best communicated where instructor and instructed stand nearly upon the same level. Even for the office of "a teacher of babes" information cannot be too extensive nor study too profound. He whose teachings stand alone, the very type and model of simplicity, was Himself the INFINITE MIND.

II.

HIS AIM.

THE teacher, who himself possesses, will see the importance of imparting to his scholars a connected and orderly view of Scripture truth. The great object of Sabbath-school instruction is undoubtedly the *conversion of souls to God*. But this end is far more likely to be secured as the result of a full and intelligent acquaintance with divine truth than by the reiteration of one ceaseless appeal. Teachers who in almost unvarying tone employ every Sabbath in urging immediate submission to God, may often succeed in arousing a transient emotion, but it is seldom, indeed, that their instructions produce the deep and lasting conviction essential to a change of character. And even where this is the case, the feeling is often superficial where it is sincere. The religion fostered by such influences is not an intelligent, deep-seated thing. A knowledge of Holy Scripture is the means appointed by God for making men wise unto salvation. "Of His own will begat he us *by the word of truth.*" Let the teacher go, therefore, steadily, earnestly on, exhibiting in order and fullness the whole counsel of God, enforcing each command and pointing each appeal in its own place, and while it is his great professed aim to enlighten the understanding, seeking to keep alive the conscience and affections of his charge by the power chiefly of his own deep sympathy and evident concern for their souls. The reason why so many forcible appeals, both in the pulpit and Sabbath-school, fail of their effect is, that care has not been taken to enlist the judgment and inform the mind. A very fervent flame is lighted, but there is no fuel.

There are two points on which, as it seems to me, the religious teaching of the young in our day is somewhat deficient. One is the bearing of Scripture principles on the ordinary duties, relations and concerns of all men. Religion is regarded too much as a thing apart. Sufficient pains are not taken to show how its holy influences were meant to be the guiding, all-controlling spirit of life. The Bible is hardly exalted to its rightful position as the Book of Humanity. The proverb, "Work is worship," is almost left to those who would assert it independently of Scripture truth. The consequence of this, both in the world and the Church, is most injurious. The piety of the one is debilitated; the carelessness of the other is confirmed. Early life is the fitting season to inculcate a higher and better view. And nowhere can it be done so effectually as in the Bible class, for human life and the Scriptures, rightly understood, are commentaries upon each other. It is but for the wise instructor to perceive and to insist upon the connection, and it will at once take its place among recognized principles in his pupils' minds. Every Scripture lesson should then be illustrated as far as possible from common life; every principle deduced from the sacred record made to bear upon ordinary duty. In the daily walks of existence, too, the instructor who does but keep his eyes open may learn much that will help him in his Sabbath work. Every scene abounds with Scripture illustrations to those who are wise enough to perceive them. "Not a household occurrence, not even a street encounter, not an anecdote in biography or an event in history, that may not, if the mind be only quick to understand and apply it, be turned to rich account in the school-room. *All that is re-*

quired, is a spirit full of its work. This will make the eye keen to perceive and the imagination swift to apply."

The other neglected point to which I refer is that of Christian evidence. "Is Christianity from God?" is a question which, though we evade it in the school-room, our scholars will be sure to meet out of doors. It is discussed in work-shop and factory with greater skill, ay and learning too, than some of us suspect. Why should not those who leave our classes be prepared to confront the objector, and give a reason for the hope that is in them with meekness and fear? That the majority of even Christian youth educated in our Sabbath-schools cannot do so now, is but too certain. They can but fall back upon the principle, "Whether he be a sinner or no, I know not; one thing I know, that whereas I was blind, now I see"—very sufficient and satisfactory for themselves, but not enough to silence objections or refute opponents. The subject demands the diligent attention of teachers. As far as possible they should familiarize themselves with the leading evidences of the truth of our holy religion, and be prepared to incorporate them, as opportunity might present itself, into the course of instruction. This should not, indeed, be done in a formal way. To devote a series of entire lessons to the topic would be likely to do harm rather than good. Especially injurious would it be to raise objections for the purpose of confuting them. In such case the doubt will often remain and the refutation be forgotten. But in almost any course of scriptural instruction there will occur many opportunities of pointing out the marks of truth and divinity which beam from every inspired page. Little heed need be taken, in such references, of probable objections; minds in which the conviction of truth is but strong and deep will be ready to meet the cavil when it comes. Occasionally, too, a particular passage may lead to a lengthened conversation on some striking point of evidence. An instance occurred a few Sabbaths ago in connection with the history of the Apostle Paul, which the class were studying. The reference in Romans xv. 25, 26, gave rise to a comparison of several passages on the same subject, exhibiting the undesigned correspondences between them, as traced by Paley in his Horæ Paulinæ. The argument founded upon this coincidence was apprehended with perfect clearness by most of the scholars, one of whom emphatically declared it to be "quite beautiful."

I pass over several more common topics. Let it not, however, be imagined that I would abate one jot of the earnestness which the pious teacher feels for the conversion of his children's souls, or would in the least deny the necessity of the aid of the Holy Spirit to render the best-devised instructions effectual. It is because that aid is promised most abundantly in connection with the wisest means, and because a thorough acquaintance with divine truth is the Spirit's mightiest instrument, that I have urged the teacher to seek first of all to impart to his scholars a full, comprehensive and intelligent knowledge of the Bible.

III.

HIS METHOD.

AFTER what has been said, it is scarcely necessary to add that in the actual labors of the class the Bible should be the text-book. Catechisms should not be taught. The order of Scripture should be preferred to the order of theology. In the younger and infant classes, indeed, I would strenuously urge the use of the simpler catechisms as presenting the elements of religion in a brief and easy style. But in the Bible class the word of God may speak for itself. The lessons to be committed to memory in the week should be mainly Scripture passages. Hymns may be added, but as a recreation, and with some restrictive care on the part of the teacher. The habit, common in some Scripture classes, of learning a great number of hymns, to the exclusion of almost every other lesson, causes great waste of time both on week-day and Sabbath, and is besides very enervating to the scholars' minds. The task is amusing at the time, custom makes it very easy, its results are somewhat showy; but no solid instruction is gained. Rapidly acquired, the sacred rhymes are as quickly forgotten, and in a few years the memory is a mere repository of scraps and fag-ends, in which snatches of merest doggerel and fragments of loftier poetry lie side by side in almost undistinguishable confusion. Still, if such a task be given occasionally as a treat, and if *perfect accuracy* in repetition be required, the exercise will be found both pleasing and useful. The state of a child's mind will sometimes suggest to the teacher an appropriate hymn, the Scripture lesson may call to mind an illustrative passage of sacred poetry, and what is learned in these or similar circumstances is likely to be well remembered and really profitable.

If the attendance of the same scholars could be secured for four or five years, it would be desirable to take the whole Bible in course, preserving strict chronological order, and taking each prominent point for a subject. But as this is an evident impossibility, the best practical plan seems to be to arrange several short series of lessons, selected both on account of their intrinsic value, and with a view to their connection with other portions of the entire scheme. These lessons, wisely chosen, will be so many centres around which the different parts of divine revelation will be *grouped*, while all are made to bear upon the point toward which all the plans of God converge—the Cross of Jesus Christ. Every course of subjects, however brief, will thus appear in its place as related to a mighty whole; some idea will be gained of the character and order of the wondrous plan; the scholars will be prepared to enter upon a new series with greater intelligence and interest, and with every fresh topic their knowledge will grow more enlarged and precise, until, either through the teachings of the class, or by subsequent instruction, they have been led to attain something like an adequate view of the whole counsel of God.

I add the titles of a few subjects which may serve as useful hints:

1. *The fifty-third chapter of Isaiah.*—Let the scholars search at home in the week for the fulfillments of this prophecy as recorded in the evangelical history, taking a few verses at a time.* The passages found will afford

---

* The natural mistakes made in searching for proofs will often be very instructive to the teacher, as affording marks of an intellectual quickness which requires only right direction. A scholar lately in a class where the above-mentioned lesson was given, took the first words of the chapter, "Who hath believed our report?" as a *question*, and assiduously sought out instances of persons who had believed the teaching of Jesus, as an answer.

topics of abundant and instructive comment. When this has been done, let similar predictions throughout the prophetic writings be sought and compared. Let some little information be added respecting each prophet to whom reference is made, as to his person, his era and his special mission. A class may thus be interested for five or six Sabbaths, attaining in the course of the lesson a general idea of the character of the prophetic line, of its great object, the "testimony of Jesus," and of the nature and design of the sacrifice of Christ. Other topics, it is plain, might be included at the discretion of the teacher, and this single chapter made to bear more or less upon every part of the revelation of God.

2. *The life of the Apostle Paul.*—Scarcely any course of lessons could be imagined more comprehensive or more instructive than this. It would indeed be rather long, but the teacher, by a careful previous review and selection of topics, might contract it almost at pleasure. Scripture history, Christian doc-

trine, the development of the law in the gospel, Christian character in its elements, and Christian life in its successive stages, would all be most fully illustrated. Add to which, that the comparison of the history in the Acts with the references in the Epistles, would be useful, not only as giving completeness to the narrative, but as furnishing powerful evidence of the authenticity of the sacred record. One of the best and really simplest defences of the truth of Christianity ever published is the Horæ Paulinæ; and a skillful teacher would have little difficulty in rendering its chief points intelligible to any average Bible-class.

3. *Sections in the history of our Lord.*— The life of Christ, taken altogether, is too long a subject. According to the arrangement of most question-books, it occupies nearly two years. This makes it somewhat tedious, especially as similar incidents often recur, and the same practical lessons are continually repeated. Parts, however, of the

evangelic history may be taken with great advantage, the study of each to occupy some eight or ten Sabbaths. A Harmony of the Gospels will be necessary, or the passages investigated may be harmonized by the teacher himself. The commencement of our Lord's ministry, down to the calling of Matthew (Matt. iii. 1–ix. 9. Mark i. 1–ii. 14. Luke iii. 1–v. 28. John i. 19–iv. 54), his last days on earth (Matt. xxi. 1–xxvii. 66. Mark xiv. 17–xv. 47. Luke xxii. 14–xxiii. 56. John xiii. 1–xix. 42), and his resurrection, with subsequent appearances to his disciples, might be mentioned as appropriate topics. A full discussion of this last subject, as actually conducted in a Bible-class, will be given in the concluding part of this volume, by way of exemplifying the principles here laid down.

Topics of practical importance, unconnected with any particular passage, might be occasionally proposed to the investigation of scholars already acquainted with the outlines of Scripture truth. To other scholars the exercise will be almost useless. They must understand what the Bible is before they will know how to look for its teachings upon any specific subject, or how to judge of their application when found. Young people, somewhat advanced, will, however, derive great profit from such research. I again subjoin one or two lessons from the actual work of a Bible class:

4. *Prayer.*—Cite passages respecting its nature, its obligation, the state of mind needful for engaging in it, its delightfulness, its appropriate topics, its special encouragements, its hindrances, evidences of sincerity in presenting it, with examples of prayer from Scripture.

5. *Outward hindrances in following the path of duty.*—I refer to this subject both because it is a very good one, and because I happen to have before me the paper texts upon it brought by a Bible-class scholar. It is subjoined, as a good specimen of what may

be expected of an intelligent, well-taught child.

"Exodus xxxii. 24. Numbers xiii. 30, 31. Deut. xiii. 6–8. 1 Sam. xv. 24. 1 Kings xix. 2–4. Nehemiah vi. 2, 3. Job xxxi. 34. Prov. i. 10; xxix. 25. Isa. li. 12, 13; lvii. 11. Jer. xxxviii. 19. Dan. i. 10; iii. 16. Jonah i. 3. Matt. xxvi. 41, 69–74. John iii. 2; vi. 66; ix. 22; xii. 42; xix. 12, 13. Acts iv. 18, 19; xxiv. 27. Gal. i. 16; ii. 11, 12. 2 Tim. iv. 16. Heb. xi. 24–27. 1 Peter iv. 14. 2 Peter ii. 1. Rev. xxi. 8."

6. *Conversion*—its need, its nature, with Scripture examples.

7. A *command* might be taken, as that in Matt. v. 44, and examples cited of obedience to it, or the reverse.

8. Or a *promise* might be given, as that in Ps. xci. 15, and instances adduced of its fulfillment. The Beatitudes would furnish a useful exercise of this kind.

Scholars yet more advanced may be encouraged to write their thoughts upon some simple question arising out of the subject that may have been discussed: as, Why was the temptation of Jesus suffered? Why did Christ appear, after his resurrection, to his disciples only, and not to unbelievers? Was it right in the apostles to elect Matthias? Was Paul ever reconciled to Barnabas and Mark after their dispute? What did Jesus mean by the sin against the Holy Ghost? One great benefit of these exercises will be that, although the scholars may not be able thoroughly to grasp the subject prescribed, their efforts to understand it will prepare them to receive with intelligence and thoughtfulness the elucidations of their teacher. In some cases they will be found unable to express their thoughts in writing. They can still be encouraged to think the question over and give their conclusions orally. The use of the pen, however, is always, where possible, to be commended; for in the words of Bacon, "Writing maketh an exact man."

The scholars themselves will often suggest

profitable subjects for conversation in the class or for study during the week. Their questionings will always be encouraged by the judicious teacher, who will only have to take care that they do not lead too far from the matter directly in hand. Many points of casuistry may thus arise, as—to refer again to inquiries actually proposed to the author in a Bible-class—Was Adam's sin forgiven? Was it right in David to pray for vengeance on his enemies? Was it not stealing for the disciples of Christ to pluck the ears of corn? Is it right to hate our father and mother? Are all rich people wicked? At some of these difficulties we may smile; yet are they sources of serious perplexity to the minds of some scholars. They ought always to be fairly met—disposed of, not sideways or by any mystification whatever, but clearly and to the satisfaction of those who propose them. Else will one or two things inevitably follow: the moral sensitiveness of our pupils will be weakened, or their confidence in the purity of Scripture principles impaired. Either result would be most deplorable; for of all things it is important both to preserve in the minds of the young an enlightened, unperverted conscience, and to show the dictates of that conscience to be in perfect harmony with every teaching of God's word.

A most useful exercise for young people who can write easily is that recommended and illustrated by Abbott in his "Young Christian," the relation in their own language of some incident in Scripture story. It would often be well to appoint this as the task for the week after the discussion of the passage in class. I say the *week after;* for the teacher's descriptions, references to locality and scenery, illustrations from other parts of the sacred record, and inference of practical lessons, will have created in the scholar's mind a far more vivid conception, and given to him, therefore, a much greater facility of expression than an unassisted examination of the passage could possibly have enabled him to attain. In this manner the biography of some eminent Scripture character might be written through, in sections; that, for instance of Samuel or of the Apostle Paul.

The manner of teaching can be scarcely prescribed. Each skillful instructor will have his own peculiar style. Generally speaking, it should be free and familiar; a conversational exposition in which the listeners should be encouraged freely to avow their difficulties and express their thoughts. First draw forth, I would say, all that your scholars know about the subject; then bring in your superior knowledge to complete their information. Avoid all formality. Take no question-book with you into the class. Use such a book, if you like, at home in preparing the lesson, but when your scholars are around you throw it aside and meet them mind to mind. You will be able to do this without difficulty if your own knowledge of the subject is clear and complete, and if you possess withal a distinct apprehension of the form in which it will be most suitable to present it to the class. The rest you may safely leave to the occasion. A very few questions, wisely put at the outset, will quicken the thoughts of your pupils to activity, and set them, most probably, in the same channel with your own. Or if they should take a different direction you will be able to follow them easily, perhaps to bring them back, or perhaps even to accompany them, for it will often undoubtedly happen that their remarks and questions will make it necessary to develop a subject in a somewhat different mode than that which had been fixed upon in a teacher's previous studies. Only take care, as I have said before, that these questions do not lead you out of sight of the matter really in hand. Digressions are often dangerous things, and though a "Let us return to the subject" may be very well in an essay or a sermon, it is sure to be somewhat distracting to the minds of a Sabbath-school class.

Let your remarks be as brief and pointed as possible. Do not discourse. If, in pursuing a description or urging an appeal, you find yourself becoming rather tedious, interpose a sudden question or stop short in a sentence that a scholar may finish it. One or two eager listeners will instantly respond, and the flagging attention of others will be aroused. Make abundant use of the Scriptures. I have seen scholars lay their Bibles aside and shut them up while their teachers were talking. This ought never to be. No matter to how many parallel passages you refer the class, so that they are really illustrative. Never bring in reflections or appeals where they are not required for the mere sake of making them. They will only be wearisome. Neither imagine yourself bound to introduce certain truths, even the most glorious, the most awful, the most fundamental, on every occasion. Insist upon them fully when the subject naturally leads to them, but do not regard it as necessary to inculcate them when it does not. "If you would imitate Christ, do not teach more than one thing at once; do not attempt to teach too much. Jesus Christ did not. He uttered a great doctrine and then dwelt upon it. He did not take his hearers through the whole field of theology at once. He was not like some preachers and teachers, who think every address should have in it 'the gospel,' which is a sure way of every address being always the same."

Should any demur to the standard set up in the foregoing pages as too high for ordinary scholars and teachers, I would only ask, with all affection, Have you ever thoroughly studied the minds of those whom you instruct? Have you ever made the attempt to guide them through a full, connected, consecutive course of spiritual instruction? Do you always, conscientiously and thoroughly, study the lesson for your class? I do not believe that any Bible teachers, who can answer these questions with an unqualified affirmative, will regard it as impossible to train the youth of our schools into an intelligent and even profound acquaintance with the counsel of God. It is time, at least, that the experiment were fairly made. The members of our churches are too generally in a state of discreditable ignorance. They may respond to the appeals of the pulpit, but they are unprepared for its instructions. Long has this been deplored; but it still remains the weakness and—might I not add?—the disgrace of the church. It is to the Sabbath-school and the Bible class that we must mainly look to remedy the defect. Let teachers but be enlightened, earnest, painstaking, impressed with the dignity of their work and filled with the Spirit of God, and we may yet see around us a generation of Christian men and women in every rank of life, who to their faith and virtue shall add the treasures of an enlightened understanding, and whose "love shall abound yet more and more in wisdom and in all knowledge."

The following conversations must speak for themselves. They are in great part intended as an illustration of the principles already set forth.

MY BIBLE CLASS.

I.

FIRST SABBATH.

THE only merit which the following dialogues claim is that of being true to the life. They are the record of hours actually and most happily spent in imparting instruction to the young. And they are presented here, not because they display any especial talent in the teacher or any extraordinary ability in the scholars, but because it is believed that they afford a fair illustration of the working of intelligent children's minds, and may therefore be useful to those instructors who would understand the material on which they have to work.

No attempt is made to report every word

that may have been uttered by the teacher or the children. Many common-place though necessary questions and answers passed, to give which would occupy space to little purpose. Sometimes, too, it was needful to "break up" the question as given here into smaller portions, to vary its form, to repeat and explain it in a manner which the experience of every practical instructor will suggest, but which it is quite unnecessary here to record. Substantially, however, the conversations are correctly given. With regard to the mode and style adopted they will sufficiently explain themselves; and the writer only hopes that the interest which they excited both in teacher and scholars may in some measure be partaken by the readers.

The class consists of thirteen girls, from eight to fourteen years of age. All of them can read well and most have been trained to think. A subject lately given them, to occupy a few Sabbaths, was "The appearances of Christ to his disciples after his resurrection."

The first chapter taken was John xx.; the scholars being directed to read in the previous week the accounts given by Matthew (xxviii. 1—10); Mark (xvi. 1—11); and Luke (xxiv. 1—12).

The chapter was first read through without the interruption of questions. This, it is believed, is the best way to secure attentive reading and complete understanding. It may be also remarked that experience shows the practice of reading from period to period to be preferable, on the same accounts, to that of taking verse by verse.

This having been done the teacher asks, "Have you read the passages from the other evangelists?"

All answer in the affirmative.

"Let the first four turn to Matthew, the second four to Mark, the last five to Luke. You will remember what you have read from John without having it open before you."

Here little Harriet, a thoughtful child of ten years old, inquires, "Teacher, may I ask a question? I have been wondering why John is so different from the other gospels."

"I am glad to hear you ask, my child. Can any of you tell me which of the four Gospels was last written?"

Susan, an elder girl, replies, "John's."

"Quite right. Now Matthew, Mark and Luke wrote nearly at the same time, in different places. Neither of them saw what the others had written. You can understand, therefore, that they would tell the same things over again and that their gospels would be very much alike. Think of something that you find in all three of them."

Two or three reply, "Suffer little children to come unto me." Susan adds, "The parable of the sower."

"Well, are these in John?"

"No, teacher."

"And can you tell me something in John that is not in the others?"

Mary Jane, who has been waiting some moments for the opportunity, instantly answers, "The raising of Lazarus." Susan repeats, half unconsciously to herself, " Let not your hearts be troubled."

"Those instances will do very well. Now I want you to see the reason of the difference. John's gospel, you say, was written a long time—"

"After the rest."

"And when the others, too, were well known by the Christians. He had the writings of Matthew, Mark and Luke before him, and so did not think it worth while to tell over again what they had given before. Do you understand the reason now, Harriet?"

"Oh yes, teacher."

"Then what must you do if you want to find out all that Christ did and said?"

"We must read all four."

"Exactly what we are going to do now. But, is everything written down which Jesus did?"

Two or three reply with a ready "Yes." Mary Jane says, "No," and leaves the matter there. Susan smiles, and begins to turn over the leaves of her book. In a few moments she reads—

"There are also many other things which Jesus did; the which, if they should be written every one, I suppose that even the world itself could not contain the books that should be written."

"Very well. I should like you to find me something before next Sunday which Jesus said when upon earth, but which is not given in any of the four gospels."

"But, teacher, where shall we look for it?"

"Why, you know there are other books in the New Testament beside these four. But now let us turn to our lesson. You can tell me, of course, who it was that went earliest to the sepulchre of Jesus?"

Several answer, "Mary Magdalene."

"But was she alone?"

Susan (with Matthew before her) reads, "The other Mary—"

Emma (with Mark),—"Mary, the mother of James, and Salome—"

Harriet (with Luke), — "and Joanna, teacher."

"What do you know about Mary Magdalene, Eliza?"

"Jesus cast out of her seven devils."

"And you can tell, Susan, who was the husband of that other Mary?"

No reply. "Look then to Matthew x. 3."

"Oh, Alpheus, because he was the father of James."

"Yes; he is called Cleopas, too. We shall read more about him by and by. This Mary was the sister of the mother of Jesus."

"Then she was Jesus' aunt," exclaimed Eliza.

"Exactly. Now what do you know about Salome?"

All are silent. "Look, then, Susan, at Matthew xxvii. 56; and you, Mary Jane, at Mark xvi. 1. Now, Susan, what three women were together?"

"Mary Magdalene, and Mary the mother of James and Joses, and the mother of Zebedee's children."

"What three do you find, Mary Jane?"

"Mary Magdalene, and Mary the mother of James, and Salome."

"Well, Fanny, put these two together: and who was Salome?"

"The mother of Zebedee's children, teacher."

"And who were Zebedee's children?"

Several reply, "James and John."

"Yes; remember there were two Jameses. Mary was the mother of one and—"

"Salome of the other."

"Which of them wrote the epistle?"

Harriet suggests, "The son of Mary."

"How do you know that, my child?"

"Because James the brother of John was killed with the sword by Herod."

"True; long before the epistle was written. He is often called James the Less: the son of Zebedee is James the Greater. But there was one other woman with the two Mary's and Salome?"

Four or five answer, "Joanna."

"And who was she?"

Fanny and Harriet turn over the pages of their Bibles; the rest seem speculating. At last the former reads, "The wife of Chuza, Herod's steward."

"Yes; as you found, my dear, in Luke viii. 3. Now Herod was—"

"The king."

"True; and what sort of a man would his steward be?"

"A wicked man," says Eliza.

"Perhaps, my dear; but I did not mean that. Would he be rich or poor?"

"Oh, rich, teacher."

"Most likely, as he was a king's treasurer. What kind of persons mostly followed Jesus?"

"The poor."

"Find me a text."

Susan turns to Matthew xi. 5: "The poor have the gospel preached to them." Mary

Jane to Mark xi. 37 : " And the common people heard him gladly."

" Yes, you see how he loved and welcomed all. He had a kind word for everybody, pity for the poor, comfort for the sorrowful, a smile for little children. The Scribes and Pharisees mocked and hated him for it, but he told them the story of the—"

" Prodigal son."

" And showed them that though they might scorn him his love made angels glad. But he did not turn away the rich. Sometimes they left him in sorrow, like the young ruler who could not give up his gold; but if they were willing to follow him he received them with the same kindness. What had he done to Joanna?"

Harriet replies, " Healed her of her infirmities."

" Right; and so she followed him from gratitude. She was not too proud, you see, to be with the poorer women of Jerusalem, who had also found Jesus to be their loving

Friend. Others were with them we know from Luke. Very likely the poor woman was there who washed his feet with tears. And they went very early in the morning; do you not read it so?"

All answer, "Yes."

"For in the chapter you have been reading from John you find that it was—"

"Yet dark."

"Yes, my dears; they were, you see, so anxious. They had not had time to bury him properly on the evening of the crucifixion, because—"

But the ellipsis was unsupplied.

"Because, you know, the Sabbath drew on. The day was always reckoned then to begin at sunset the evening before. But now the Sabbath had passed, and like a company of weeping sisters they went in sadness to the tomb. As you sometimes sing—

'Sweet spices they brought on their star-lighted way
And came to the grave at the dawning of day.

'But who will the stone from the sepulchre roll?
They said, as the tears from their weeping eyes stole.

'The stone is removed, and the Saviour is gone!
Oh hail, ye disciples this bright Sabbath morn!'

But the school bell rings. We must finish talking about this chapter another time."

Eliza smilingly observes, "We have only got through one verse yet, teacher."

"True, my dear; but you see even one verse may lead to a great many things and be very full of the love of Christ. And now let us go together into the house of God."

II.

SECOND SABBATH.

THE first question, when the scholars were again assembled, related to the saying of Jesus " not given in any one of the four gospels," for which they had been directed to search. But all were at fault. Susan, Harriet and two or three more had evidently tried hard to find it, but had discovered no clue. The others looked as though they had altogether forgotten the request. It became necessary, therefore, to refer them to Acts xx. 35: "Remember the words of the Lord Jesus, how he said, It is more blessed to give than to receive." After a few remarks suggested by this passage, which it is needless to record, the subject of the last Sabbath was resumed; three of the children turning to Matthew, three to Mark, three to Luke, four to John. The reading for once was omitted, as the class were already familiar with the four accounts, and as the introduction of another passage might have disturbed the unity of impression.

None had forgotten who the women were who went together so early to the sepulchre of Jesus.

"And what did they talk about by the way?"

"About Jesus," exclaimed little Lucy, the youngest of the class, an ardent, bright-eyed child. Some smile, as if they thought a subject of conversation could not have been wanting, but made no reply. Mary Jane reads from Mark: "They said among themselves, Who shall roll us away the stone from the mouth of the sepulchre?"

"You can tell me, then, how the sepulchre was formed?"

"It was a cave in the side of the rock, teacher."

"Yes; and the stone was fixed in the front, like a door. How was it fastened?"

"It was sealed," two or three reply. Susan adds, "I should not have thought sealing would have been of much use to a stone."

"Think a moment, my dear. Why was the seal placed there?"

"That the disciples might not steal away the body of Jesus."

"Yes; or rather that if they did they might be found out. The Jews did not want so much to make the stone fast as to show if any one rolled it away. So they put a broad band or ribbon across the front and sealed it to the rock on each side. If, then, the disciples had come and taken away the stone—"

"They would have pulled the ribbon away and broken the seals," cries little Harriet, eagerly.

"To be sure; and so the Jews would have known in a moment—"

"That the disciples had been there."

SECOND SABBATH. 55

"But, teacher," says Charlotte, an intelligent, earnest child, whose voice it is quite a treat to hear, she speaks so seldom, " were not the *women* afraid of breaking the seal?"

" Do you think, my dear, they knew it had been put there?"

The question seems to perplex the scholars. They consult their Bibles, but no solution appears.

"Well, on what day was the stone sealed up?"

Susan reads from Matthew xxvii. 62: "On the next day that followed the day of preparation."

"And what day was that?"

" The Sabbath."

" Quite right; and where were the women on the Sabbath, Fanny?"

Fanny answers from Luke xxiii. 56: "They returned, and rested the Sabbath day, according to the commandment."

" True. You see they had left the Saviour's grave to keep God's day. They did not know that the enemies of Christ had been breaking the Sabbath in fastening up the sepulchre, or, very likely, they would not have been so bold."

"There were soldiers at the grave too, were there not, teacher?" asked Eliza.

"What makes you ask, my child?"

"I have seen them in pictures, teacher."

"But we must have better reason than that."

"There were 'keepers,'" Susan says, referring to Matthew xxviii. 4.

"And they are called in the 12th verse—"

"Soldiers."

"Just as Eliza said. Do you think the women knew of them?"

All reply in the negative.

"Why do you think not?"

"They would have been afraid to go," says Lucy. Mary Jane adds, "The soldiers were set there on the Sabbath too, teacher."

"But now, while these poor women were on their sorrowful way, what had happened?"

Four or five reply, "Jesus had arisen."

"Read me the verse, Emily, which speaks of this."

Emily reads Matthew xxviii. 2.

"Does this describe how he arose?"

"Yes, teacher." "No, teacher." Susan adds, in a moment, "It only tells what the angel did."

"True, my dear. I suppose that Jesus left his grave in so wonderful and glorious a manner that it could not be described. We know that when the angel, with face like lightning and raiment like snow, rolled away the stone, the keepers—"

"Did shake and become as dead men."

"And then the Son of God came forth unseen. All that the women found when they came up was that—"

"The stone was removed and the Saviour was gone," murmurs Susan.

"Were the soldiers gone away?" asked Fanny.

"You can answer that, Emily?"

"Yes, teacher, they were gone to the city, to the chief priests."

"True; another time we will talk of the tale they made up. But now tell me whom the women saw at the empty grave."

"The angel who rolled away the stone," says Susan, referring to Matthew.

"A young man sitting on the right side, clothed in a long white garment," reads Mary Jane from Mark.

"Two men in shining garments," Harriet answers from Luke.

"And these men in shining garments were—"

"Angels from heaven."

"Yes; they put on this appearance that the women might see them. How many did you say there were?"

"Two." Mary Jane inquiringly suggests, "One."

"Ah! you find that Matthew and Mark say one, Luke two. Now which do you think is right?"

SECOND SABBATH. 59

"Both of them, teacher," says Eliza.

"How so, my dear?"

"If there were *two* there must have been *one*," was the smiling reply.

"Exactly so; but why do you think Mark and Matthew only mention one?"

A moment's pause. Mary Jane then suggests, "It was only one *who spoke.*" Susan adds, "They do not say there were *no more* than one."

"Quite right, my children;* and the one who spoke, told the women—"

"That Christ had arisen."

"Joyful news, indeed! Did Mary Magdalene hear it?"

"Yes, teacher."

"Are you sure of that? Where did the women see the angels?"

"At the sepulchre."

---

* Just so Mark and Luke mention the cure of only one Gadarene demoniac; Matthew speaks of two. The two former, again, describe only one blind man as healed at Jericho; Matthew shows that two were restored to sight.

"Outside?"

"No, teacher; they were inside."

"True; and did Mary Magdalene go in with the other women? Harriet, you have John open; tell me."

"No, I do not think she did."

"But why do you not?"

"She ran away directly she saw the stone rolled from the sepulchre."

"Yes, Salome, and Joanna, and Mary the mother of James, went in to see if they could find out the meaning of this wonder, and there the angels met them. Mary Magdalene was too much astonished to stay, but turned round and went as fast as she could to—"

"Peter and John."

"And what news did she take to them?"

"That Jesus had arisen," answered Fanny. "No," says Susan, "that he had been carried away."

"Yes, Susan is right. Read the second verse, Lucy."

Little Lucy reads John xx. 2.

"I need not ask you who was this disciple whom Jesus loved?"

All reply, "John."

"Why do we not read his name?"

Two or three look as if they could reply, "It is not for us to say." Susan is thinking. Harriet exclaims, "Because John wrote the verse himself." Susan, with a bright smile of discovery, adds, "He was modest and did not like to mention his own name."

"A very good lesson to vain people! But now we have only a minute or two longer, and I want to ask you about one thing more. Were John and Peter by themselves or with the other disciples?"

"By themselves."

"Yes; and I should like you to think of a reason. What sort of a man was John?"

"Loving," one replies; "Gentle," another; "Kind," a third.

"How did he show it?"

"He leaned on Jesus' bosom," says Mary Jane. Charlotte whispered to herself, "He wrote a great deal about love." Eliza, blushingly eager to display her lore, relates the anecdote of the aged apostle carried into the assemblies of the Church when disabled by infirmity from all other service and saying, when he could say no more, " Little children, love one another."

"And what had Peter been doing a little while before?"

"He had denied Christ three times."

"Was he sorry for it?"

"Oh yes, teacher." Harriet repeats, "He went out and wept bitterly."

"Ah, he was in sad trouble. And when we are sorrowful to what sort of persons do we like to go?"

"To those who will be kind to us."

"We do, indeed! and so Peter left the other disciples after his great sin and went alone with the gentle and loving John. I dare say the rest were angry and would have nothing to do with an apostle who had done so wickedly. But John would speak tender words to him and cheer his troubled heart. 'I am sure Jesus forgave you, dear Peter, before he died. God will pardon and love you still if you trust in him. Do you not remember the parable of the lost sheep? and what our Master said once about the bruised reed? Think of these things, seek your Father in heaven and be comforted. So they spent the Sabbath by themselves together: and the next day Mary brought her wonderful news.'"

"How glad they must have been!"

"I am not sure of that, my dear, for they did not yet know what had really happened. Next time we must talk about what these two disciples did and perhaps shall see a little more of Christ's love to Peter. And try if you can find out for me in the week in what part of the Bible it is said, 'There is a Friend that sticketh closer than a brother.'"

III.

THIRD SABBATH.

THE worship of the school to-day was commenced by the hymn,

> "There's a friend above all others,
> Oh how he loves!
> His is love beyond a brother's,
> Oh how he loves!"

Two or three of the scholars exchanged glances, as though the subject of the hymn were in harmony with their thoughts. It was clear that they remembered Peter and had found the text which the reference to him on the preceding Lord's day had suggested. Accordingly they were no sooner seated in class with their Bibles in their hands than several turned to Proverbs xviii. 24, and listened with an earnest attention that proved a previous interest in the subject, while a few simple words were spoken of "the Friend that sticketh closer than a brother." The tears came into little Harriet's eyes as she said, turning to Mark xvi. 7, "The angel spoke of Peter, too, teacher."

"He did, my child; you can tell me to whom?"

"To Salome and the woman who went into the sepulchre."

"Yes, while Mary Magdalene was hastening away to the two disciples. The angel told these women also to go, but with better news than Mary could take. Read what he said, Mary Jane."

"'He is risen; he is not here: behold the place where they laid him. But go your way, tell his disciples *and Peter* that he goeth before you into Galilee: there shall ye see him, as he said unto you.'"*

* Mark xvi. 6, 7. Mark is generally thought to have been Peter's companion and to have written under his

"And why do you think Peter's name was mentioned so particularly?"

"To let him know that he might come with the rest," says Eliza. "To show that he was forgiven," answers Susan.

"Very true, my dears. It was a message of love from Jesus himself. John had done quite right in comforting him. The lost sheep might again unite with the 'ninety and nine,' and all be happy in the care of the One Shepherd."

"But the women *did not* go to Peter," Charlotte timidly suggests.

"No, my dear; Mary Magdalene had already taken him very different news. I do not think the other women knew that he and John were away from the rest. So they went to the other disciples, expecting to find them all together, but very soon after they had left the sepulchre, there came running up—"

direction. The grateful heart of the apostle no doubt fixed with especial emotion upon these two words of the angelic message, and though unrecorded by the other evangelists, he could not forget them!

"Peter and John."

"Both together?"

"No, teacher, John first."

"How was that, do you think?"

The class seemed perplexed, and unable to tell.

"Which, then, was the elder of the two?"

"Oh, Peter," Susan replies, "and John ran quickest, because he was the younger."

"How far had they to go?" asks Mary Jane.

"I cannot exactly say, my dear; most likely not more than half a mile. But when John came up, what did he do?"

"Stooped down and looked in."

"And Peter, when he came?"

"Went into the sepulchre."

"Yes, right past his companion, with breathless haste, unable to stay till he had discovered all! How came John to remain outside?"

"I should think he was afraid, teacher," replies Eliza, with a smile.

"Very likely, my child: gentle people, you know, are often very timid. But Peter was always—"

"Brave," "Quick," "Eager," "Zealous."

"Now, then, which of the two characters do you like best?"

The question gives rise to a difference of opinion which it is curious to observe. The majority are at once for the "beloved disciple." Eliza, Mary Jane, with one or two more, incline to Peter. Susan, who always keeps her judgment under a certain degree of control, is evidently balancing the rival excellences, and can scarcely decide between them.

"Perhaps, my dears, it is best to be a little like both; brave and earnest, like Peter, when we are quite sure we are in the right; and always gentle and affectionate in temper, like John. It would be hard perhaps to tell which of them loved the Saviour more, or which felt the deeper sorrow when they found, as they thought, that even his body was taken from them."

"I wish they had met the other women," says Harriet.

"Ah, they would have heard wonderful things then! But they might not perhaps have believed them. The rest of the disciples did not, as we shall see by and by. Tell me now what Peter saw in the sepulchre."

Fanny reads John xx. 6, 7: "He seeth the linen clothes lie, and the napkin that was about his head, not lying with the linen clothes, but wrapped together in a place by itself."

"And what clothes were these?"

"The grave-clothes of Jesus," answers Fanny, referring to ch. xix. 40.

"How were they laid together, Lucy?"

"Quite tidily, teacher."

"True; and can you think, Susan, of any reason why John tells us this?"

Susan evidently has a glimpse of the right reply, but it is not clear enough for expression; she only looks eager, colors and is silent.

"You remember what the Jews said afterward had been done with the body of Jesus?"

"That the disciples had stolen it away while the soldiers slept."

"Do you think they were bold enough to do such a thing?"

"No, teacher," two or three at once reply. Susan quickly turns to Matt. xxvi. 56 and reads: "Then all the disciples forsook him and fled."

"Yes, and that was when he was first taken. How much more cowardly would they have been after his death! But supposing they really had attempted after all to take his body away, in that bright moonlight night, with the soldiers lying round, and close by the city that was full of his enemies, do you not think they would have been very much frightened?"

All assent. Susan exclaims: "They would never have stayed to fold up the linen clothes." Fanny adds, "They would have been in too

THIRD SABBATH. 71

great a hurry to stop a minute, for fear the soldiers should wake!"

"Very true; and thus you see the folded grave-clothes were quite a proof that the disciples had not done as the Jews said and that the rising of Christ had been as calm as it was mighty. But did John remain all this time outside?"

"No, teacher; he went in to Peter."

"He soon heard Peter's voice calling from the inside of the sepulchre, 'Come in, come here and see what marvelous things have happened.' His fearfulness all vanished away, and he too went in and saw—"

"And believed."

"Yes; and what was it they believed?"

"That Jesus had arisen?" says Mary Jane, inquiringly.

"Yes, my dear, I think they did, though we are not exactly told. You know what they had believed before?"

"That the Jews had taken him and laid him somewhere else."

"What made them change their minds?"

"Was it the grave-clothes, teacher?" quietly hints Charlotte.

"What would they learn from them, my child?"

"If the Jews had taken him away they would have wanted the clothes to carry him in," replies Charlotte.

"Quite true. I have no doubt Peter and John thought of this: and do not you think they remembered anything beside?"

"What Jesus had said, teacher," answers Fanny.

"Can you find any text in which he foretold his death and resurrection?"

After a little search, and a very little assistance, Emily finds Matthew xvii. 23; Mary Jane, Mark ix. 31; Harriet, Luke ix. 22; and Susan, John ii. 22. The passages are read.

"The apostles, I dare say, recollected these words, and so were filled with joy. But do not any of you think that by searching they might have learned the same thing in another way?"

No answer is given for a few moments. Charlotte then suggests, "The Old Testament prophecies."

"Exactly so; and did Peter and John think of these? Read the ninth verse."

"'For as yet they knew not the Scripture, that he must rise again from the dead.'"

"What Scripture?"

"The Bible, teacher."

"All the Bible?"

"No; only the Old Testament."

"For the New was not yet written. I should like you in the week to look for the passages of the Old Testament that prophesy the resurrection of Christ. If you cannot find many, one or two will do, and we will read them next Sunday before we go on to talk of the appearances of Christ to his disciples. What joy it would have given if they had but understood those texts earlier! But they never thought of their meaning. And even while John and Peter were together in the empty tomb, and had just begun to believe the wonderful truth that Jesus had arisen from death, they did not recollect what David had said, or Isaiah, or Hosea. They only judged by what they saw there and by what they remembered hearing from Jesus. It was not till afterward, when Jesus himself explained it to them, that they understood how clearly their own scriptures had said that Christ must die and rise again." *

* The ninth verse is generally urged against the view of the apostles' "belief" given above; and the sum of their conviction is supposed to have been that *the body of Jesus had been removed.* But this they believed before: it was a matter obvious to their senses. The faith spoken of was evidently the result of examination and reflection. The apostle seems desirous, in pursuance of his great design (xx. 31), to mark the precise moment when the belief he commends to others took possession of his own mind. The ninth verse points out the fact that his belief was based entirely on his own consciousness and experience—very decisive indeed, but without the fullness and certainty which it afterward attained, when he "knew the Scripture," and comprehended the whole divine and glorious plan.

"He called them 'fools, and slow of heart to believe,'" said Susan, referring to Luke xxiv. 25.

"He did, my dear; but we must talk about that walk to Emmaus another time. How did Peter and John act when they left the sepulchre?"

"They went away again unto their own home."

"Yes, to wonder and pray and wait until their risen Master should appear. But there was one who could not leave his tomb."

"Mary Magdalene."

"She had come up after Peter and John, unable to keep up with them, as she was wearied with running to their house to take them her news before."

"I wonder they did not meet her as they left the sepulchre," says Mary Jane.

"They must have gone away by a different path. We know that they did miss her, or they would have told her their joyful belief, and removed the grief that she felt so deeply,

She came slowly, sadly on, I fancy, for still she thought—"

"That the body of Jesus had been taken away."

"And so she waited, weeping there, anxious to find—"

"Where they had laid him."

"Or, if no one appeared to tell her this, she could at least watch the place where he had been, and think of his love better by his grave than anywhere else, though her heart was almost broken."

"I wish Peter and John had met her," says little Harriet, her eyes filling with tears again.

"Ah, my child, she was soon to see a better, greater One than they. You know what happened. But I see it is time to close. Next Sabbath we must talk of the way in which her sorrow was turned into joy. We shall see too how the other women were blessed and comforted, and how all the friends of Jesus shared in his remembrance and his love."

IV.

FOURTH SABBATH.

THE list of Old Testament prophecies concerning the resurrection of Christ, brought by the scholars, was not very large. Some had discovered but one text; and the only passages adduced at all were Psalm xvi. 9, 10, and Hosea vi. 2. A few simple comments were made upon these texts, designed to show their double application, to type as well as antitype. One of the children afterward asked, "Are there no more prophecies, teacher? I was surprised to find so few."

"Not exactly of the resurrection, my dear; but there are many passages that foretell the glory that Jesus should inherit after his sufferings. This glory began—"

"When he rose from the dead."

"Yes; and so of course every text that speaks of his greatness and kingdom is a prophecy of his resurrection too.

The scholars soon caught the idea, which was further illustrated by reference to Psalms cx. 1, ii. 7 (compared with Acts xiii. 33), and Is. liii. 12. The subject of last Sunday was then resumed.

"You remember where Mary Magdalene was when we left her?"

"By the tomb of Jesus, weeping."

"And as she wept—"

"She stooped down and looked into the sepulchre."

"Whom did she see?"

"Two angels in white."

"What angels were these?"

"The same that the other women had seen before."

Eliza, with characteristic quickness, inquires, "How was it Peter and John had not seen these angels?" Mary Jane suggests,

"They had gone away before the apostles came up, and now came back again to Mary." Susan, however, reminds us, "They were spirits."

"And what then, my dear?"

"They could become unseen, teacher, whenever they chose."

"True, or rather they would be always unseen, unless God commanded them for some good purpose to reveal themselves. Angels, we know, are around us day and night, but we never see them."

Fanny repeats, "He shall give his angels charge over thee, to keep thee in all thy ways." Little Lucy half whispers to herself,

"I lay my body down to sleep.
Let angels guard my head."

"These bright beings, then, had been in the sepulchre all the time, but only showed themselves to the women. What did they ask Mary?"

"Woman, why weepest thou?"

"Ah, she thought she had reason enough

to weep, and almost wondered at the question. But what did she say?"

"Because they have taken away my Lord and I know not where they have laid him."

"Her heart was full of this. She thought of nothing else, and did not seem to fear or even to wonder at the sight of angels. Did they answer her?"

"No, teacher; she turned away directly."

"Hearing a rustle, perhaps, behind her; and there was standing—"

"Jesus."

"How was it she did not know him?"

The question seems a perplexing one. At last Susan bethinks herself of the first verse and replies, "It was yet dark."

"True, my dear, when the women first went to the sepulchre. It must have been lighter now; but it was still early and perhaps only twilight. Then, you know, her eyes were dim with tears. Besides, are you sure she looked at him so as at all to notice who he was?"

A pause.

"Turn to the 16th verse."

"Oh no, teacher, she was looking another way," replies Charlotte.

"How do you know that, my child?"

"Because afterward, when she knew him, she *turned herself* to speak to him."

"An excellent answer! and that shows—"

"That she was not looking 'straight at him' before."

"True; she only saw in the dim light that *some one* was standing there; she thought it was—"

"The gardener."

"And so, without caring to observe him particularly, only asked him her one most anxious question—"

"Sir, if thou hast borne him hence, tell me where thou hast laid him and I will take him away."

"And then Jesus said unto her—"

"*Mary!*"

"One word! It was enough! That old

voice! So sweet, so gentle, so full of love! The glorious truth rushed instantly over her mind. Jesus had arisen indeed, and here he was to bless her! In a moment she had fallen at his feet, and in her new wonderful surprise could only utter one single word—"

"*Rabboni!*"

"My Master! The tears fell fast again, but now it was a joyful weeping. She clasped his feet and would not let him go. But what did Jesus say?"

"Touch me not, for I am not yet ascended to my Father."

"Do not cling to me now, for I am not yet going to leave you. You will have other opportunities of seeing me before we part. I have an errand for you. Loose me, therefore; go and tell my brethren—"

"I ascend unto my Father and your Father, and to my God and your God."

"Did she go?"

"Oh yes, teacher."

"Faster, I dare say, even than when at

first she ran to Peter and John. Overjoyed, glowing, breathless, she was soon with the disciples; and how did they receive her wonderful tale?"

"They believed not," replies Mary Jane, reading Mark xvi. 10, 11.

"Ah, John and Peter were not with them yet; and the news seemed too good, too glorious, to be true. But had any others brought it besides Mary Magdalene?"

"Yes, Salome and the other women."

"Had they seen Jesus too?"

"Yes, teacher," replies Emily, referring to Matthew xxviii. 9, 10.

"When we last spoke of them they were—"

"Going away from the sepulchre to the disciples."

"Who had sent them?"

"The two angels."

"And this was just before John—"

"Came running up with Peter behind him."

"And Mary Magdalene behind them both. Then, while these women were on their way—"

"Jesus met them and said, 'All hail.'"

"That is, welcome; rejoice and be glad. And how did they feel?"

"They were afraid."

"Strange, was it not, when the angel had said to them that Christ had arisen? Mary Magdalene was not afraid when she saw Jesus, though none had told her he had left the grave. Perhaps Mary had a little more faith than Salome and her companions."

"But they fell at his feet, too, teacher, and worshiped him."

"True, my dear, but with a little terror; for he had to say to them, 'Be not afraid,' before he sent them to his disciples. What command were they to give them?"

"To go into Galilee, and they should see him there."

"Did the disciples believe what these women said?"

"No, teacher," answers Fanny, reading Luke xxiv. 11: "Their words seemed to them as idle tales, and they believed them not."

Here Harriet, who has been quietly thinking for some minutes, exclaims, "Then Christ appeared to the other women before Mary Magdalene saw him?" "No," answers Mary Jane, "for Mark says (xvi. 9), 'he appeared first to Mary Magdalene.'" "But," rejoins Harriet, "they went away from the grave a good while before Mary Magdalene came up the second time."

"Harriet is right, I think. When Mary saw Jesus, they had already reached the disciples with their tale of wonder, and she came in afterward, most likely before they had left, to say what she, too, had seen."

Mary Jane, however, is decidedly unconvinced, and still appeals to the authority of Mark.

"I do not think, my dear, that the text you read just now proves that Harriet and I are wrong. Mark says, 'first to Mary Magdalene,' because it is the first appearance of the risen Saviour *that he has recorded.* You see he mentions only three."

"First to Mary; after that to two as they walked into the country; afterward unto the eleven as they sat at meat."

"True; Mary Magdalene saw him the first of these three times. Mark does not say that Jesus appeared to her first *of all.* And if we put together Matthew's account and John's, we shall see that at first Salome with her companions met him as they were hastening from the sepulchre to the disciples, and that then, secondly, he came to Mary at the grave.* But next, and thirdly, he appeared—"

---

* "A main difficulty occurs in fixing the order of time between our Lord's appearance to Mary Magdalene and that to the other women. This arises from the use of the word *first,* in Mark xvi. 9, which seems to imply that this appearance to Mary Magdalene was the first of all. Yet the whole course of events and circumstances shows, conclusively, that Jesus had pre-

FOURTH SABBATH. 87

"To the eleven in Galilee?"

"To the eleven in the evening as they sat at meat?"

"To the two disciples going to Emmaus?"

"All wrong, my dears. There was one appearance before any of these—a very gracious and loving one, though we do not read much about it. But we have not time to

viously appeared to the other women. We are, therefore, compelled, and that in accordance with good and ordinary usage, to regard '*first*,' as put here, not absolutely, but relatively. That is to say, Mark narrates three and only three appearances of our Lord; *of these three*, that to Mary Magdalene takes place '*first;*' and that to the assembled disciples, the same evening, occurs 'afterward,' or, as the word should properly be translated, '*last.*' Hence, as '*last*' is here put relatively, and therefore does not exclude the subsequent appearances of our Lord to Thomas and in Galilee, so, too, '*first*' here stands relatively, and does not exclude the previous appearance to the other women. Similar examples are found in 1 Cor. xv. 5–8 and in John xxi. 14. In this way the whole difficulty in the case before us vanishes; and the complex and cumbrous machinery of earlier commentators becomes superfluous."—PROFESSOR ROBINSON.—*Harmony of the Gospels.*

seek it out now. Try to discover it before next Sabbath; and when we then come together, I hope you will all be able to tell me who it was that saw Jesus next after Mary Magdalene on that wonderful first day of the week."

V.

FIFTH SABBATH.

"THERE is an account of the appearances of the risen Saviour that we have not yet consulted. You can tell, Susan, where it is to be found?"

"In the fifteenth chapter of the First of Corinthians."

"Say, rather, of the First *Epistle to the* Corinthians, my dear. We will read, then, first of all, a part of that chapter."

The scholars turn to it accordingly. Mary Jane smilingly remarks, "I have found the answer to your last question there, teacher."

"Ah, I hoped you would! But now we will read down to the 28th verse."

The chapter is read as usual, from period to period, the teacher taking turn with the scholars.

"Now, then, Mary Jane, what was the question?"

"To whom Jesus appeared next, after Mary Magdalene."

"And to whom was it?"

Three or four of the scholars simultaneously reply, "To Cephas. To Peter."

"Yes, here it is in the 5th verse. It is the first appearance that Paul mentions. But how do you know when it happened?"

After a few moments' silence, Harriet suggests, "There is another text that speaks of it, teacher."

"True, my child; read it to us."

She has already turned to Luke xxiv. 34, and now reads: "The Lord is risen indeed, and hath appeared to Simon."

"By whom was this said?"

"By the eleven apostles."

"And to whom?"

"To the two disciples who had returned from Emmaus."

"At what time in the day?"

"In the evening."

"Had the eleven seen Christ themselves when they said it?"

"No, teacher."

"Then Peter alone had met him. Most likely about the middle of the day, after the appearances to—"

"The women and Mary Magdalene."

"Well, and what account have we of their conversation?"

"None at all, teacher. No one else was with them."

"Can you think at all what it was likely to be?"

"Jesus would speak kindly to him," says Charlotte, in a low tone.

"Ah, my dear, you remember what we said about Peter before. He needed comfort. John had given it like a loving friend; but the Friend that sticketh closer than—"

"A brother."

"Yes, *closer than a brother*, remembered the disciple who had so deeply sinned, so bitterly repented; and determined to give his consolation too. Can you imagine why Jesus did not meet Peter first with the other disciples?"

"It would have shamed him too much," suggests Harriet.

"True, my child. We see how gentle and thoughtful was the blessed Jesus. He knew that Peter could scarcely believe himself forgiven his great sin, and met him, therefore, apart, where none of his companions could too closely watch his sorrow or disturb his grateful joy. Just as he himself had commanded his disciples to act to one another."

"I know," says Susan, repeating the passage: "If thy brother shall trespass against thee, go and tell him his fault between him and thee alone; if he shall hear thee, thou hast gained thy brother."

"And truly Peter was 'gained' by such love. Never did he forget the tenderness of the Saviour; and his whole life seemed to say what his lips soon after uttered three times so earnestly—"

"Lord, thou knowest all things; thou knowest that I love thee."

"But now we will go back to the account in the gospels. Where shall we find the next appearance recorded?"

"In Luke xxiv."

"And—"

"In Mark xvi. 12," replies Emily, reading: "After that, he appeared in another form unto two of them, as they walked, and went into the country."

"To what place?"

"The village of Emmaus."

"How far from Jerusalem?"

"Threescore furlongs—seven miles and a half," adds Susan.

"Do you recollect in which direction?"

"The north-west, I think, teacher," answers Mary Jane, and a reference to the map, which is always at hand, proves her reply to be correct. The village, it is added, is now so utterly ruined that its exact site is now uncertain.

"And who were the two disciples?"

"Cleopas and another." Little Lucy adds: "Please, teacher, do you know who the other was?"

"No, my child, not exactly, but—"

"I should think it was Luke," exclaims Susan.

"Why so, my dear?"

"He would have told the name if it had been any one else."

"Then do not the sacred writers mention their own names?"

Two or three answer, "John does not."

"Very true, and Luke is like him in this. So, Susan, many learned men have had just your thought upon the matter. But it is not of great consequence either way. You all know who Cleopas was."

Three or four, remembering the first lesson, reply, "The same as Alpheus." "The husband of Mary." "The father of James." "Of James the Less," subjoins Mary Jane, who likes to be correct.

"One of them lived at Emmaus, perhaps both. They had been to Jerusalem to keep the feast—"

"Of the passover."

"And had lingered past its close, in hope perhaps of hearing something that might explain the strange, sad events which had so unexpectedly taken place. Or perhaps they waited in the thought that even yet their sorrow might be turned into joy. But now they had given up all hope, and were sadly returning home. How did they pass the time as they walked along?"

"They talked together of all these things which had happened."

"No wonder, for their hearts were full. They could think of none but Jesus—the happy days they had spent with him; his countenance of tender love; his voice like gentle music; the wonderful truths he had taught them; the glorious hopes he had inspired. Would they had prized these blessings more! For now they were over and gone; the hope and joy all buried in his grave! But surprise and gladness were preparing for these disciples, of which they little dreamed. For while they communed together and reasoned—"

"Jesus himself drew near and went with them."

"But they did not know him. How was that?"

Emily referring to Mark, answers, "He appeared in another form."

"Exactly. It was a miracle. He had not in reality risen with a different body, but he chose to change its appearance. His first question was a natural one from a seeming stranger, ignorant of the subject of their conversation."

"What manner of communications are these that ye have one to another as ye walk, and are sad?"

"But see how surprised Cleopas was at the question."

"Art thou only a stranger in Jerusalem,

and hast not known the things which are come to pass there in these days?"

"As if they could have been speaking on any subject but *one!* Were there many strangers in the city at that time?"

"Yes, teacher; attending the feast of the passover."

"Right. Alpheus thought their new companion must be one of these. No one who knew the place could possibly be ignorant of the events of Calvary. But Jesus only asked—"

"What things?"

"And then they began to tell him, both almost at once. It was a relief to them. First Cleopas, who speaks of Jesus of Nazareth as—"

"A prophet mighty in deed and word before God and all the people."

"Ah, he did not, after all, understand the real greatness of the Saviour's work. He thought only of the wonderful teachings and the mighty miracles; and these made it so hard to understand how Jesus could ever have submitted or how God could have suffered him to die. For, after speaking of his death, he adds—"

"We trusted that it had been He which should have redeemed Israel."

"And were they not right?"

"Yes, teacher." "No, teacher."

"You are both correct, my dears. Jesus did come to redeem Israel, but not in the way they had thought. I often told you what the Jews expected him to be."

"An earthly king."

"Yes, to redeem them by his wisdom and might from their earthly oppressors, whose arbitrary rule was so galling to every Jew. You know who these were."

"The Romans."

"And when, therefore, he was seized and put to death, every hope seemed utterly destroyed. They thought of no other redemption; they 'trusted' once; they could trust no longer now! But Cleopas, and very likely his companion too, speaking both together,* go on with their story—"

"Beside all this, to-day is the third day since these things were done. Yea, and certain women also of our company made us astonished, which were early at the sepulchre; and when they found not his body, they came, saying that they had also seen a vision of angels, which said that he was alive. And certain of them which were with us went to the sepulchre and found it even so as the women had said, but him they saw not."

"How eagerly and wonderingly they spoke! and how sorrowfully too! It was past their understanding. They could not make it out."

"I do not think I should have gone away from Jerusalem if I had been in their place," observes Susan.

* The disjointed, hurried way in which the latter part of their account is given quite suggests this idea. It is just the style in which two persons, strongly excited, would jointly, breathlessly, tell their artless tale.

"Why so, my dear?"

"I would have waited to see whether what the women said were true."

"Ah, and they would have remained if they had at all believed the news. But the very thought of a resurrection seemed impossible."

"Did they think the women told a *story* about the angels?" persists Susan.

"Not quite so, my dear; but very likely they thought the women were deceived by fancy, and only dreamed that they saw angels in the morning twilight."

"I am sure they would never have gone to Emmaus if they thought Jesus could have risen," adds Harriet.

"Exactly what I said, my child. But now the truth in its glory was to be made known. How surprised they must have been when their unknown companion says in reply to their mournful account—"

"O fools, and slow of heart to believe all that the prophets have spoken! Ought not

Christ to have suffered these things and to enter into his glory?"

"Teacher," says little Lucy, "did not Christ say it was very naughty to call anybody a fool?"

Mary Jane turns to Matthew v. 22. The class look in silence for an explanation.

"Yes, my child; those who give this or any other bad name to their companions, in anger or hatred, are in danger of hell fire! But you do not think the blessed Jesus was angry?"

"Oh no, teacher."

"Certainly not! He only wished to show his disciples that they were '*thoughtless*' (the true translation). You know I sometimes call you the same, when you have not attended to what you have been told."

"Not very often, teacher, I hope," little Lucy rejoins, with a winning smile; and she was right.

"Well, my dear, these disciples had been thoughtless. They had not attended to what the prophets had clearly said. And in a most beautiful manner Jesus now goes on to show them what things had been written concerning himself. Try and find out some of these prophecies. We will begin with them, and finish the story next Sabbath, for now it is time to close our books."

VI.

SIXTH SABBATH.

WHEN the class had assembled, it was perceived that four or five of the scholars had their Bibles already opened at Isaiah liii. Their thoughts had evidently been resting on this solemn prophecy as the likeliest theme of conversation in that walk to Emmaus. It was, therefore, thought appropriate that the chapter should, in the first place, be read. No sooner was it concluded than Eliza exclaimed,

"Did not the two disciples know of this chapter before, teacher?"

"Most likely they did, my dear; but why do you ask?"

"They could not have *helped* seeing that Jesus must die."

"Ah, my child, remember how full their thoughts were of the expected kingdom. This led them to explain the prophecies altogether in a mistaken way. All promises of glory and greatness they applied to their coming king; but when the prophet spoke of sorrow and death, they thought the words must mean some one else. I dare say they would have been quite shocked, before Jesus made it clear to them, to have been told that this fifty-third of Isaiah was written about the Messiah, the King of Israel."

"Whom did they think it meant?" inquired Susan, very naturally.

"That is a thing I cannot tell. Perhaps they applied it to Isaiah himself. You recollect the question once asked about this very passage by a nobleman traveling through the desert, sitting in his chariot."

"I know," exclaims Mary Jane, turning to Acts viii. 34: "'I pray thee, of whom speaketh the prophet this? of himself or of some other man?'"

"Yes, Luke and Cleopas perhaps had often asked the same question. But never once had they thought of the true answer. How beautifully it was now made known! Do you remember what their feelings were as they walked and listened?"

"Their hearts burned within them."

"Yes: you can well understand that. What wonder! what delight! what love! 'How comes this stranger, whom we have never seen with Jesus, to know so much more than we do?' 'Who can he be?' 'Strange that we never thought of this before!—*despised and rejected of men!* how exactly that describes our beloved Master!—*as a lamb to the slaughter!*—oh yes, we well remember how patiently he stood!—*taken from prison and from judgment!*—ah, we saw him and wondered that the angels of heaven did not come down and deliver him!—*with the rich in his death!*—the tomb of Joseph where now he lies!' But they listened on to the wondrous unfolding of Scripture prophecy until they understood that he had left that tomb. For the prophet speaks of victory and glory too."

"'I will divide him a portion with the great, and he shall divide the spoil with the strong,'" reads Susan.

"And again it is said, 'He shall see of the travail of his soul, and shall be satisfied.' This also was explained to the disciples, until their sorrow was turned into brightest joy by the conviction that their Saviour, though he died, had conquered, and now had arisen a king indeed! But this was not all their unknown companion unveiled to them. For what purpose did Jesus die?"

"To save sinners," several reply. Charlotte, more thoughtfully, says, "To make a sacrifice for sin." Susan quotes the passage, "Christ hath once suffered for sins, the just for the unjust, that he might bring us to God."

"And do you not think Jesus spoke of these truths too? Might he not have found them in this very prophecy?"

"Yes, teacher, the fifth verse—'He was wounded for our transgressions, he was bruised for our iniquities: the chastisement of our peace was upon him! and with his stripes we are healed.'"

"This, indeed, must have completed the disciples' astonishment and joy. 'We thought him our king, we find him our Saviour! We dreamed of his living to give us thrones on earth, we see that he died to gain for us crowns in heaven! He was delivered for our offences, and—'"

"Raised again for our justification."

"But this chapter of Isaiah was not the only prophecy that Jesus explained?"

"No, teacher, I found three others," says Mary Jane.

"Let me hear them, my dear."

"One was Psalm xxii. 1: 'My God, my God, why hast thou forsaken me?'"

"How do you know that refers to Christ?"

"He said the very words upon the cross."

"True. It was a solemn and a mournful

cry. But for him we must all have uttered it for ever. Had not he borne our sins, God must, in righteousness, have forsaken *us* to all eternity."

"The second passage is in the sixty-ninth Psalm, teacher."

"But are there no other words of prophecy in Psalm xxii.?"

"Yes, teacher," exclaims little Harriet, reading verse 18: "They part my garments among them, and cast lots upon my vesture."

"Exactly. You recollect that this was one part of the shame that Jesus suffered when crucified. But now, Mary Jane, will you read your second text?"

Mary Jane reads Psalm lxix. 21: "They gave me also gall for my meat; and in my thirst they gave me vinegar for drink."

"Yes, you recollect that this is spoken of as the last prophecy that was fulfilled in the death of Christ. Can any of you turn to the passage?"

The scholars seemed perplexed. Perhaps

the question was rather ambiguous. They are, therefore, referred to John xix. 28–30. "You see that when the vinegar had been given Jesus said—"

"It is finished."

"And in those words what did he mean to declare?"

"That all things were now accomplished."

"And the SCRIPTURE FULFILLED. But you spoke of a third passage, Mary Jane."

"It was Zechariah xii. 10: 'They shall look on me whom they have pierced.'"

"Very right. And these words are applied in the New Testament to—"

"The piercing of Jesus with the spear."

"In what passage?"

"In John xix. 37," replies Mary Jane, reading the verse.

"Is there no other text where the words are quoted?"

After a few moments' busy search, Susan and Charlotte simultaneously light upon Rev. i. 7.

"Were these all the prophecies that you think Jesus explained to the two disciples?"

"Oh no, teacher. They were all I was able to find," adds Mary Jane. "I found two more," says Charlotte quietly.

"And which were they, my child?"

"One was in Daniel ix. 26: 'And after three-score and two weeks shall Messiah be cut off, but not for himself.' The other was Zechariah xiii. 7: 'Awake, O sword, against my shepherd, and against the man that is my fellow, saith the Lord of hosts.'"

"I am glad, my dear, that you have been so attentive. But all the prophecies you have found speak of the sufferings of Christ. Did Jesus talk of nothing else in that walk to Emmaus?"

"Yes, teacher, of entering into his glory."

"True; this was most needful to encourage and gladden the disciples' hearts. But once before you brought me predictions from the Old Testament on this subject. No doubt the Saviour spoke of them all. Do you not recollect one very striking passage: The Lord said unto my Lord—"

"Sit thou on my right hand, until I make thine enemies thy footstool," continues Susan quickly, soon discovering the words in Psalm. cx.

"Yes; and when these prophecies and those which told of sorrow and death were brought together, how beautifully and wonderfully they explained each other! showing that the Son of God died as a sacrifice and rose as Prince and Saviour. But, Susan, you have not brought any passages. How is that?"

"I began to look, teacher, but could not get on."

"Indeed, but did you not think of those texts in the Psalms that Mary Jane and your sister Charlotte have read?"

"No, teacher, I did not get so far as the Psalms."

"Not so far! Then where did you begin, my dear?"

"Luke says that Jesus began at *Moses*,

and so I tried to find prophecies of Jesus there."

"And you might have done so in Gen. xxii. 18; xlix. 10; Num. xxiv. 7; Deut. xviii. 15."

"Not of his sufferings and death, teacher."

"True; but you know Jesus spoke of 'all things concerning himself.' Still, there is one prophecy recorded by Moses which certainly was fulfilled in the death of Christ. The. first promise—you recollect it?"

"Oh, about the woman's seed and the serpent, in the 3rd chapter of Genesis," exclaims Susan, quickly finding out the passage.

"Exactly. The seed of the woman refers, you know, to—"

"Jesus Christ."

"The serpent is—"

"Satan."

"And on the cross Satan was permitted to put forth his power against the Saviour. Jesus so declared it himself. Do you remember the passage?"

All are silent.

"'The prince of this world cometh, and hath nothing in me.' Satan seemed to conquer for a time, for Jesus died, and was laid in the grave. It was as though his heel was wounded, and he was overthrown. But Christ arose, death was conquered; he that had the power of death, that is, the devil, was subdued, and the serpent's head was crushed. A glorious prophecy gloriously fulfilled! I can imagine that Jesus began with this; so going onward from the very first, bringing every prophet in turn to give witness how Christ, the great Deliverer, should first suffer, be slain, then rise victoriously and reign in heaven. But there is one other way in which Moses spoke of Christ. You told me, Charlotte, just now, that the Saviour died as—"

"A sacrifice for sin."

"And was not this truth set forth before he came into the world?"

"Oh yes, teacher, by the sacrifices of the law."

"And whom did God send to give that law?"

"Moses."

"True, and in Christ that law was fulfilled. So that there was much to speak of here. The disciples had often seen the sacrifices in the temple, often watched the blood of sprinkling flow, often partaken of the passover lamb; but never till now had they known what these things should mean. Oh, with what surprise and rapture must they now have heard of the sacrifice which was thus set forth; the 'precious blood of Christ,' the 'Lamb of God, that taketh away the sin of the world!'"

"I never thought of the sacrifices, teacher," says Susan.

"But now you see, my dear, that even in Moses there is much that sets forth the work of Jesus, and that might well have employed the whole of that long and happy walk. How sorry Alpheus and his companion were when the scattered roofs of Emmaus at last appeared before them! Was it possible? How short the furlongs had been! But now they had reached the door. Their stranger friend is saying good-bye!"

"He made as though he would have gone farther," reads little Lucy.

"Was not that *pretending?*" interposes Emily.

"What do you think of it, my dear?"

"I know it is wrong to pretend," Emily replies. Harriet steps in to relieve the difficulty, and says, "The disciples *thought* he was going farther, teacher."

"True, my dear, and their thought is set down here, not the thought that was in the mind of Jesus. It appeared to them that their companion was bound for some place beyond; and certainly he would have gone on had they not pressed him to stay. So there was no pretence in the matter, dear Emily. But they could not bear to say farewell just yet. What invitation did they give?"

"Abide with us, for it is toward evening, and the day is far spent."

"It could not have been *very* late, for they had another walk the same evening."

"Yes, they returned to Jerusalem."

"Seven miles and a half more. Then before that they had to dine. But the Jews reckoned evening to begin at three o'clock; and very likely it was now about that time. Did Jesus go in?"

"Oh yes, teacher."

"And sat for a time, still conversing and partaking of their meal. How glad they must have been to entertain one who had discovered to them such glorious things! But how overwhelmed with wonder and delight when, at last—"

"He took bread and blessed it, and brake, and gave to them, and their eyes were opened, and they *knew him*."

"It was He! The words of blessing, the

old familiar action, revealed the truth! No stranger, then, after all, but the Lord, the risen Lord! They were dumb with astonishment. Nor did he speak more, but he looked upon them for an instant with one smile of tender, infinite love, and then was gone! For a few moments longer they gaze silently upon his vacant place; and then we seem to hear the half whisper of one to the other, as if unable to recover from the awe of that strange surprise: 'Did not our hearts burn within us while he talked with us by the way, and while he opened to us the Scriptures?' But there was no time to lose. Others must know these wonders too. Nay, they could not stay. So they arose from their couches and girded up their robes again, and fastened on their sandals—"

"And returned to Jerusalem—"

"Talking by the way, of we can imagine what! Ready to stop every stranger they met and tell him the news! Never had the sixty furlongs seemed so long! But the walk was finished at last, and they burst breathless into the disciples' room. But, before they had time to speak, the apostles had met them with a tale almost as wonderful as their own—"

"The Lord is risen indeed, and hath appeared to Simon."

"And now for the present we must leave them there. I think there is just time left to read you some lines on the subject of which we have been talking:

> It happened on a solemn eventide,
> Soon after He that was our Surety died,
> Two bosom friends, each pensively inclined,
> The scene of all those sorrows left behind,
> Sought their own village, busied, as they went,
> In musings worthy of the great event;
> They spake of Him they loved; of Him whose life,
> Though blameless, had incurred perpetual strife;
> Whose deeds had left, in spite of hostile arts,
> A deep memorial graven on their hearts.
> The recollection, like a vein of ore,
> The farther traced, enriched them still the more;
> They thought him, and they justly thought him, one
> Sent to do more than he appeared to have done—

To exalt the people, and to place them high
Above all else, and wondered he should die.
Ere yet they brought their journey to an end,
A stranger joined them, courteous as a friend,
And asked them, with a kind, engaging air,
What their affliction was, and begged a share.
Informed, he gathered up the broken thread,
And, truth and wisdom gracing all he said,
Explained, illustrated and searched so well,
The tender theme on which they chose to dwell,
That, reaching home, "The night," they said, "is near,
We must not now be parted—sojourn here."
The new acquaintance soon became a guest;
And, made so welcome at the simple feast,
He blessed the bread, but vanished at the word,
And left them both exclaiming, "'Twas the Lord!
Did not our hearts feel all he deigned to say,
Did not they burn within us by the way?"

"What beautiful verses!" exclaimed Susan. "I should like to learn them, teacher; may I?"

"Assuredly, my dear; I will write them out for you, and bring you the copy next Sunday."

"May I learn them, too?" adds little Harriet.

"Ah, you want another copy, I see! Well, I will give one to every scholar who will promise, next Sabbath, to commit the lines to memory in the following week. I see from your looks that, if you continue in your present mind, I shall have no small amount of writing to do!

"But now we must close our books and go into the house of prayer."

VII.

SEVENTH SABBATH.

ON the next Sabbath the application for the lines quoted from Cowper were very numerous. Two or three of the younger children held back, because "they could not read writing very well;" but the production of a few copies, written in Roman characters for their especial use, soon changed their hesitation into delight. All promised to commit the verses to memory, and it was plain that they would keep their word.

"I am sure, my dears, you all remember where we left the apostles last Sabbath."

"Together, in their upper room." "The two disciples from Emmaus," Susan continues, "had just come in."

"And now they were telling each other

their wonderful story. 'He has appeared to Simon.' 'He has broken bread with us.' It was a happy company! But, now, can you tell me exactly who were there?"

"The eleven apostles."

"All of them?"

"No, teacher, Thomas was away."

"And were any there beside the apostles?"
No answer.

"Will you turn then to Luke xxiv. 33, Mary Jane?"

"Oh yes, teacher, I see now. 'The eleven and them that were with them.'"

"True; and are we told at all who these others were? I see you do not just now recollect. Is there no passage that speaks of the same company as together after the Saviour's ascension to heaven?"

In a few seconds, Susan and Charlotte have both turned to Acts i. 14, and the former reads, "with the women and Mary, the mother of Jesus, and with his brethren."

"You perceive there may have been a

large party. All who loved Jesus must have felt anxious to be together. You know they were afraid, as they had good reason to be, of his enemies."

"The door was shut," says Harriet, "for fear of the Jews."

"And then they must have longed to talk with each other on the scenes through which they had passed, to weep and wonder and pray together. But yet from what happened afterward I cannot think the *women* were there. You will see what I mean directly. Mark, you perceive, describes the party as—"

"The eleven as they sat at meat."

"And John?"

"The disciples."

"And Luke as Mary Jane just now read?"

"The eleven and them that were with them."

"Then in the very midst of their conversation—"

"'Jesus himself stood in the midst of them.'"

"And what was his salutation?"

"Peace be unto you."

"Yes, Luke and John both record the same words. How did the disciples feel when they heard them?"

"Glad," says little Lucy, referring to John xx. 20. "No," says Susan, "they were terrified and affrighted."

"Quite right, Susan; the gladness came afterward, as we shall see. At first they thought—"

"That it was a spirit."

"Strange, was it not? Here these disciples had been talking of nothing else but the resurrection of Jesus; they heard that the women had seen him; Peter had told his story; Cleopas and his companion had related theirs. 'The Lord is risen indeed,' is the joyful assurance of every heart. At that moment, the same day, at evening, the doors being shut, the Saviour suddenly appears in their midst; and they are terrified and affrighted, and suppose that they see a spirit."

"I suppose they thought so because the door was fastened," suggests Mary Jane.

"Most likely, my dear; yet surely they might have known enough of the Saviour's power not to be surprised at even a miracle like this."

Here a smile on the countenance of two or three of the elder girls betokens a bright thought within. At last, Susan exclaims, "I see now why you did not think the women were there, teacher."

"Why so, my dear?"

"Because if they had been, *they* would never have been affrighted."

"Exactly. Mary Magdalene, we may be sure, could not have forgotten that morning in the garden, but would joyfully have recognized her Lord."

"But some of the other disciples there had seen him too," hints Eliza.

"True; there were Peter and the two from Emmaus. If they could doubt, the women may possibly have been as weak. Yet I can hardly think it. At any rate, we see how slow of heart the disciples were to think that their Master had arisen, so that unless it had been made quite plain and certain to them they never would have believed it. How did he prove to them that it was indeed himself?"

"He showed unto them his hands and his feet." "His hands and his side," Harriet adds, from John.

"And said—"

"Behold my hands and my feet that it is I myself; handle me and see; for a spirit hath not flesh and bones, as ye see me have."

"Did they then believe?"

"Yes, teacher." "No," says Emma, reading from Luke—"they believed not for joy, and wondered."

"Ah! I suppose that means that they could *scarcely* think it real. It seemed even yet, though they saw Jesus plainly before them, too glorious to be true. You know what that feeling is?"

A ready smile gives assent. "But did the Saviour show them in any other way that it really was he?"

"He took a broiled fish and a piece of a honey-comb, and did eat before them."

"Yes, and so they became quite sure. And *then*, Lucy, they were—"

"Glad when they saw the Lord."

"Think, now, what a happy party they must have been! Their trouble all seemed over. Jesus was sitting with them again. His words were beautiful and loving as ever. How they must have gathered round to listen! But did he find fault with them at all?"

Here Charlotte, who has long had her New Testament open at the last chapter of Mark, reads, "He upbraided them with their unbelief and hardness of heart, because they believed not them which had seen him after he was risen."

"Yes, they surely needed reproof, yet from our knowledge of his love for them we can imagine how gently and tenderly he would give it. But soon he began to speak of more welcome subjects, and said again—"

" Peace be unto you."

" Luke tells us what followed."

" He opened their understanding, that they might understand the Scriptures."

" How Cleopas and his friend, yet lingering in the room, must have felt while Jesus thus uttered over again those glorious truths which had made their hearts to 'burn within them by the way!' To what parts of Scripture did he refer?"

" The law of Moses and the Prophets, and the Psalms."

" Yes; you know I told you once that the Jews divided their Bible into three parts—"

" The Law, the Prophets and the Holy Writings."

" And the Holy Writings contained—"

" All excepting the Law and the Prophets."

" Which was the principal book of the 'Holy Writings?'"

"The Psalms, teacher."

"Yes, my dear; as I told you, it was always placed first. So that sometimes the whole collection was called 'the Psalms.' It is so here, 'the Law, the Prophets and the Psalms' is the same as—"

"The Law, the Prophets and the Holy Writings." Mary Jane adds, "The whole of the Old Testament."

"Quite right. Far into the night no doubt they sat listening, while in words such as never man spake their risen Saviour brought all the holy men of God who in old time were moved by the Holy Ghost to witness—"

"That it behooved Christ to suffer and to rise from the dead the third day."

"And now the prophecies had come to pass! But how was the news to be made known?"

"By the preaching of the apostles."

"Where is this declared?"

Eliza reads from Luke, "That repentance and remission of sins should be preached among all nations, beginning at Jerusalem."

Emily, from Mark, "Go ye into all the world, and preach the gospel to every creature." Susan, from John, "As my Father hath sent me, even so send I you."

"Different words, you see, but the same thing. Where did the Saviour command his disciples to begin their work?"

"At Jerusalem."

"Can you think of any reason for this?"

"It was their own home,"* replies Charlotte.

"True, my dear; was there anything in Jerusalem that made its inhabitants worthy of the privilege?"

"No, teacher; I should think they were the unworthiest."

"Why so, my child?"

"Because they had crucified Jesus."

"And yet you see he does not withhold his mercy. How beautifully this shows the Re-

* True, the apostles were Galileans; but as Jerusalem was the metropolis of the whole land, the above answer may be received as correct.

deemer's graciousness to even the chief of sinners! We know that the apostles did begin at this guilty city, and you remember how many were at once converted?"

"Three thousand."

"Ah, my children, it was a fulfillment of the Saviour's dying prayer, 'Father, forgive them,' and a glorious proof that he is able to save unto the uttermost. But we must go back to our histories. What powers were the disciples to have for their great work?"

Emily reads Mark xvi. 17, 18. Harriet refers to John xx. 22: "He breathed on them, and said unto them, Receive ye the Holy Ghost; whosesoever sins ye remit, they are remitted unto them; and whosesoever sins ye retain, they are retained."

"Did the apostles *then* receive the Holy Ghost?"

"No, teacher, not until the day of Pentecost."

"Quite right; and the Saviour's breathing on them was just a sign of 'the mighty rushing wind,' which another day would fill the room where they were sitting."

"But, teacher," inquires Susan, "could the apostles forgive sins?"

"Why do you ask, my dear?"

"Because we are told that none can forgive sins but God."

"True; and God gave to the apostles a spirit of wisdom and power by which they could certainly tell whose sins God had pardoned. They could, therefore, truly and assuredly say, as Jesus often said, to the penitent, 'Thy sins are forgiven thee.' Not with the power of Jesus, but as the messengers of God, enabled by the Holy Ghost to know whom he had pardoned. This would enable them to speak in the full confidence that what they bound and loosed on earth was bound and loosed in heaven. Not because they themselves did it, but because they had power to know what *God* had done. Can you find the passage where this promise about binding and loosing is given?"

In a moment or two Susan has turned to Matthew xviii. 18. After reading the words, she asks again, " Have ministers this power now ?"

" No, my dear, no more than they can perform the miracles spoken of in the verse we just now read from Mark. Wonderful gifts were needed then, which ministers do not now require. This they can still say with fullest confidence, that *whosoever* truly repents will be forgiven for Christ's sake, leaving it to the Searcher of hearts to discover who the really penitent are. The passage is quite clear to you now, I think ?"

" Oh yes, teacher."

" And was the Saviour's promise to be fulfilled immediately ?"

" No, teacher—the apostles were to tarry at Jerusalem."

" Until—"

"They should be endowed with power from on high."

" Another day we may see how they obeyed

this command. But now it is time for us to close. Next Sabbath we shall have to talk a little about the apostle who was not there."

"Thomas."

"Yes; I am sure you will not forget him! How much he lost by being away! Never had the disciples spent so happy an evening. It seemed as though they could have stayed for ever. But at last the time of separation came. The Saviour bade them farewell, and left them to wait and pray until the first day of the next week, when he would see them again.

"Now I hope that when we next meet, those lines about the walk to Emmaus will be perfectly repeated by every one. My labor then in writing them will be fully repaid."

VIII.

EIGHTH SABBATH.

AT the next meeting of the class, some time was occupied by the repetition of Cowper's lines on the Walk to Emmaus. Not one of the children had failed to learn them: they were, for the most part, repeated very accurately; while the subdued tone of some and the eager manner of others showed, according to their varied dispositions, that the power and pathos of the story were still felt.

"And now let us go back to that evening when the risen Saviour and his disciples sat so happily together. You know that one of the apostles was not there."

"Thomas, called Didymus."

"Yes, Thomas the Twin. The word Didymus means twin."

"Then, was he somebody's twin-brother?" inquires little Lucy.

"Most likely, my dear. And was he told of the visit of Jesus?"

"Oh yes, teacher! The other disciples said unto him, 'We have seen the Lord.'"

"Ah, it was news they could not keep to themselves. I dare say they told him the whole story from beginning to end: the coming in of Jesus through the unopened door; their fear and unbelief; then their gladness and praise; the gracious words of their Redeemer; and all the joys of that most happy night. Did Thomas believe them?"

"No, teacher."

"Why, how was that?"

"He said, 'Except I shall see in his hands the print of the nails, and put my finger into the print of the nails, and thrust my hands into his side, I will not believe.'"

"Was not this unbelief very wonderful?"

Two or three immediately reply, "Yes,

teacher." Susan remarks, "The other disciples did not believe at first, though they saw Jesus."

"True, my dear; and if they did not believe their own eyes it was not wonderful that Thomas should not believe *them*."

"You told us once, teacher, that the apostles doubted because it seemed too good to be true."

"Exactly. And so Thomas doubted. When Jesus died, he had given up all for lost; and now he was afraid to believe the good news, for fear he should be disappointed again."

"Was Thomas a good man?" inquires Mary Jane.

"What do you think about it, my dear?"

"I think it was very wrong not to believe *all* the disciples, teacher."

"Yes, it seems strange, certainly. And, if he had had more knowledge he would have seen there was good reason why their account should be true."

"Did the disciples tell him about the Scriptures that Jesus had explained?" interrupts Susan.

"No doubt they did. But he had made up his mind in sadness that it could not be true; and so their words went for nothing. 'We saw and heard him,' they said. 'Ah, yes! but you may have been deceived. Did you touch him?' 'No, we certainly did not.' 'Then I am not satisfied. Except I put my hand upon his very wounds, I cannot believe.'"

"I think he was rather obstinate," says Harriet.

"More likely very fearful, my dear. Some people, you know, are more timid than others. And I have known little girls, before now, afraid to hope for something that they would have dearly loved only lest they should be disappointed."

A ready smile shows that the scholars, who had become eager in attention, and were evidently trying, in their way, to solve the enigma of the apostle's character, had at once apprehended the illustration.

"But now to Mary Jane's question: 'Was Thomas a good man?' Let me ask you another. Did he love Christ?"

The class seem rather surprised at this turn, and wait as if to see their teacher's precise aim.

"I think you know of a passage that will help you to answer at once. There was a time when Jesus seemed in great danger; his enemies were determined to kill him. So he went away from Jerusalem, and lived for a time quietly at Bethabara. But he was sent for to come back to the bedside a dying friend. And the disciples were afraid and begged him not to go. Jesus was still determined—"

"I know!" exclaimed Susan, Mary Jane and Charlotte, simultaneously, quickly turning to John xi., and referring to verse sixteenth.

"And what do you find there, my dears?"

"Thomas said unto his fellow-disciples, 'Let us also go that we may die with him.'"

"True; I am very glad you remember the passage. It shows plainly what sort of man he was. You see he loved Jesus so well that he could willingly die with him. His companions may have wished to stay behind, lest the Jews, who sought to stone Jesus, should put them to death also. But 'No,' said Thomas, 'we will all die together.'"

"That was brave," half whispers Charlotte. She is evidently thinking of the description before given of Thomas as "fearful."

"Yes, my dear: he was not afraid to die, although he was afraid to hope. See, too, in the passage you just found, he seems quite sure that Jesus would be put to death. Why did he not believe that Christ would be delivered from his enemies?"

"Jesus had said," Mary Jane observes, "that he was going to waken Lazarus out of sleep."

"Yes; Thomas might have thought of this,

and been comforted by recollecting his Master's power. But no! he could only remember the malice of the Jews, and so gave Jesus up for lost—just as he did again, when the disciples spoke of his resurrection. But it was the same love that made him say, then, 'Let us go, that we may die with him;' and now, 'I will not believe.'"

The children say nothing, but look as if they would ask, "How can that be?"

"I know a little girl, whose mother was lately very ill. When I went to see her, I found the dear child quite certain that her mamma would die. Everybody told her that she would most likely soon be well; but she would not believe any of them, and mourned as if her parent were dying. And at last, when her dear mamma did get well, it seemed as if she could scarcely believe it. Do you think that little girl loved her mamma as much as her brothers and sisters did?"

"Yes, teacher, more."

"Very likely, indeed. I am sure she

could have done anything for her mother—could have died for her even—though she so soon gave up hope. Do you understand the matter now?"

A quick smile and more than one glistening eye gave instant answer. Lucy, with a look of sympathy, exclaims, "How glad the little girl must have been when she saw her mamma really well!" Harriet adds, "She would be sorry, then, that she did not believe what the others told her."

"Just so, my dears; and was it not so with Thomas? When did Jesus give him the proof that he asked for?"

"Eight days after."

"Yes, that is, on the first day of the next week."

Susan is evidently whispering to her next companion, "That would be only seven days."

"Speak out, my dear. I see your difficulty. But count both the Sundays, and then you have the eight days. The disciples had already taken the day of Christ's resurrection as their time of meeting together. And how did Jesus come?"

"The doors were shut, and he stood in their midst and said, 'Peace be unto you.'"

"Just as he did before. But what did he next say?"

"He told Thomas to reach out his hand, and feel his hands and side."

"How gracious he was, even to his disciples' doubts! He knew that Thomas loved him, and so gave him the very proof he asked for. But he gently reproved him too—"

"Be not faithless, but believing."

"Yes; Thomas should not have given way to such fears. They had cost him a miserable week! He might have had as much love, with more hope, and he would have been much happier. I dare say, now, with all his joy, he felt rather ashamed as he stood there before the disciples and remembered his unbelieving words. But was he satisfied?"

"Oh yes!"

"How did he show his faith and love?"

"He answered and said unto him, 'MY LORD AND MY GOD!'"

"To whom did he say this?"

"To Jesus."

"What did he show, then, by giving him this great name?"

"That he believed."

"Believed what?"

"That Jesus had risen."

"Nothing more?"

"That he was GOD."

"Exactly so, my child; and was this belief true?"

"Yes, teacher."

"Are there any other passages that prove it?"

Four or five of the scholars begin to turn over their Bibles; others seem considering.

"Well, we will leave this question till next Sunday. Try and find, in the week, as many passages upon this subject as you can, and bring them to me then. Was Jesus pleased with the faith of Thomas?"

"He said, 'Thomas, because thou hast seen me thou hast believed.'"

"Yes, the Saviour graciously accepted and approved his disciple's confession. But there are some, he says, more blessed still."

"They that have not seen, and yet have believed."

"And who are these?"

"All Christians."

"Yes, all who have not, like the apostles, seen Jesus himself, and yet believe in him. Can you tell me a text that speaks of such?"

Emily turns to 1 Peter i. 8: "Whom having not seen, ye love; in whom, though now as yet ye see him not, yet believing, ye rejoice with joy unspeakable and full of glory."

"Why are these most blessed?"

"Because their faith is strongest," suggests Susan.

"True, my dear. It is a small thing to believe what we see—that is, trusting to our own eyes; but when we trust only to the word of God, and receive as true what he says, although we cannot ourselves judge of it, we possess true faith and show the spirit which he approves."

"I should like to have seen Jesus on the earth!" exclaims Eliza, who has been silent an unusually long time.

"Ah, my dear, I do not wonder that you think so. Very delightful it must have been to accompany him as he went about doing good, to listen to his words of love, and, like these disciples, to meet him after his resurrection! But you know there were many who did not care for him even then."

"I could never have been like them."

"Do not be too sure, my child. Ask rather whether you truly seek and love him now; then your faith will lead you to know more of him than even these apostles knew on that first day of the week; for they had not even yet found out that he had died for their sins."

"Had they not teacher?" interrupts Susan.

"No; this they only knew when the Holy

Ghost came into their hearts at the day of Pentecost. So we are better off than the disciples of Jesus themselves when he was by them. But it is time to close. You thought just now, Eliza, of a line in a favorite hymn,

> 'I should like to have been with them.'

Remember the next verse,

> 'But still to his footstool in prayer I may go,
> And ask for a share in his love;
> And if I thus earnestly seek him below,
> I shall see him and hear him above.'

For if we trust and love him here, a time will come when we shall see him face to face, and dwell in his presence for ever."

IX.

NINTH SABBATH.

THE task which had been given to the scholars on the past Sabbath, namely, to collect Scripture proofs of the deity of Christ, turned out to have been somewhat difficult. At the next meeting of the class few were prepared with any passage at all; and of the texts which Susan, Mary Jane, and even little Harriet, had cited, some were not very relevant. All three, however, referred to John i. 1: "The Word was God;" two quoted Rom. ix. 5: "Christ, who is God over all, blessed for ever;" two Isa. ix. 6: "His name shall be called the mighty God;" and Susan also adduced Isa. vi. 1, evidently with some confused notion of the application of this sublime passage to the Messiah by the Apostle

John (xii. 41). She could not, however, recollect the evangelist's quotation, and it took a little time to make the matter clear.

On the whole, it appeared that to have prescribed such a subject was a mistake in judgment, and that the scholars would far more effectually apprehend this great truth by means of incidental reference in the course of their Scripture lessons than by any attempt to deduce it in a formal doctrinal style from a separate examination of the Bible.

The subject of the resurrection of Christ was then resumed for the last time but one.

"All the appearances of Jesus, of which we have yet conversed, were at Jerusalem; but the next was a long way off—"

"In Galilee, teacher."

"How came the apostles to be there?"

"Jesus had commanded them to go," says Emily, referring to Matt. xxviii. 10.

"True. And now, after a week's waiting at Jerusalem, they had taken the journey. In what part of Galilee did Jesus meet with them first?"

"On a mountain," Emily answers, from Matthew; "By the sea of Tiberias," says Susan, referring to John xxi.

"Well, here we have two appearances; but which of them was first?"

There is no reply. Even Emily and Susan are silent.

"Look then to John xxi. 14."

"'This is now the third time that Jesus showed himself to his disciples.'"

"That is, to the apostles. And this appearance was—"

"By the sea of Tiberias."

"Now how many times had the apostles seen Jesus before they went into Galilee?"

"Twice."

"Then this interview with them by the sea of Tiberias must have been the next after those which we have already spoken of at Jerusalem, and therefore earlier than that on the mountain. You understand it now?"

"Oh yes, teacher. Else it would have been the fourth."

"Exactly. How many disciples were together?"

"Five." "Oh no, seven."

"And who were they?"

"Simon Peter, Thomas, Nathanael, the sons of Zebedee—"

"That is—"

"James and John, and two other of his disciples." "Please, teacher," inquires Eliza, "who were these other two?"

"I cannot tell, my dear; it is not written. How were they passing their time?"

"In fishing."

"Yes; that was the way they earned their living. And they did quite right, while waiting for Jesus, to spend the time industriously. But how did they get on?"

"They caught nothing all night."*

* As an example of unreported answers, this may be given: "How was it that the disciples caught nothing?" "Because the fishes were all asleep," replied little Lucy.

"The night was the best time for their work, as the fish are attracted by the lights; but the disciples must have been weary and disheartened enough when the morning came and they found they had lost their rest for nothing. Then, as the twilight began slowly to spread, they looked from the ship toward the shore and saw—"

"Jesus."

"But they did not know him. How was that?"

"It was too dark, teacher, to see plainly."

"Exactly so; but Jesus called to them and said—"

"Children, have you any meat?"

"Yes; or as we might say, 'My good friends have you caught anything?' Of course they answered, 'No,' but did not know him yet. How came they to discover him?"

"He told them to cast in the net again, thus prompting them to renowed effort, and they should find. So they did cast it in.

And it was filled directly. Then John said to Peter, 'It is the Lord!'"

"How did Peter act then?"

"He girt on his fisher's coat,* and jumped into the sea, and came straight to Jesus."

"Yes; you see John's loving eye discovers Jesus first; but Peter's zealous heart, more fearless, brings him earliest to the Saviour's side. And the other disciples?"

"Soon came up in their ship, dragging the net after them."

"How soon their weariness was changed into busy gladness! What did they see when they came to land?"

"A fire of coals, and fish laid thereon, and bread."

"How the fire came there we cannot tell. Perhaps Jesus had himself caused it, to show that he could supply their wants now, if he chose, just as he fed the five thousand in the

---

* "For he was naked," adds the Scripture account. Rather, he was "stripped," as we say, that is, he had thrown off his upper garment, just as rowers or cricketers do now, that his limbs might have freer play.

wilderness. But he did not choose. He intends his people to work for their living. So he said—"

"Bring of the fish which ye have now caught."

"See how Peter runs to obey the command! Till now he had remained beside his Lord, and let his companions bring up the net themselves, as well as they could. But in the instant that Jesus speaks the word he is at the sea-shore, and by his single arm drags the burden to land. Well, we must pass on. Jesus says to the wondering apostles—"

"Come and dine."

"Rather, 'come and breakfast' (the Greek word refers to the morning repast, and not to the mid-day meal); for you know it was not dinner-time yet. So they sat down together. The disciples surely were very happy; but there was something that kept them silent."

"None of them durst ask him, 'Who art thou? knowing that it was the Lord.'"

"They waited, therefore, in reverence, till

he should show them himself why he had come to them there. They did not wait long. For when they had dined, or breakfasted, he asked one of the party a question—"

"Simon, son of Jonas, lovest thou me more than these?"

"Now why did he ask this of Simon and not of the rest?"

"Because he was sure of *their* love," Harriet replies. "Because Peter had denied him," adds Mary Jane.

"Ah, Harriet, Jesus was as sure of Simon's love now as of Nathanael's, or Thomas', or John's. You remember the meeting of Peter and the Saviour alone on the resurrection day. But the other disciples were not so sure. They knew that Peter had repented, but very likely they questioned whether he was quite forgiven—whether Jesus would allow him to be an apostle any more. So the Redeemer wished to make this quite clear to them—to show his love to Peter, and Peter's love to him; and to let the disciples see that, though Simon had greatly sinned, he was not to be hindered from doing his Lord's work, because he had truly repented. But you will understand this better in a little while. See how Jesus reminds him of his denial. How many times is the question asked?"

"Three times." "And," Susan quickly adds, "he had denied Jesus three times."

"Just so. It was a gentle way of reminding him that he had thrice said of his Saviour, 'I know him not.' Simon must have felt this deeply. You read how sorry he was."

"Peter was grieved because he said unto him the third time, 'Lovest thou me?'"

"And yet it was kind and gracious of the Saviour to give him an opportunity to declare his love thus openly as many times as he had uttered those words of guilt. Jesus thus would show himself,

'Though thrice denied, yet thrice beloved.'

There was another thing, too, that must have made the apostle feel. By what name did Jesus call him?"

"Simon, son of Jonas."

"This was not his only name?"

"Oh no, teacher—'Peter.'"

"And who gave him this second name?"

"Jesus."

"What is its meaning?"

Two or three scholars reply, "A rock."

"Why was it given?"

"To show that he was to be steadfast in the faith," replies Charlotte.

"Exactly so, my child; and you see why Jesus does not call him Peter now."

It is clear from the scholars' look of quick intelligence that they have caught the idea. Mary Jane alone speaks: "He had lost his steadfastness."

"Ah, 'the rock' had fallen! so the Saviour calls him by his old name—the name he had before he knew or followed the Lord. 'Simon, son of Jonas'—as though he had said, Can I call you Peter any more? Yes, if your love is true, I may—I will'—'LOVEST THOU ME?' And Simon said—"

"Lord, thou knowest that I love thee."

"Three times?"

"Once he said, 'Lord, thou knowest all things; thou knowest that I love thee.'"

"Very earnest, you see; but how humble! He does not lean to his own understanding now. He trusts to the Saviour's knowledge of his heart. There was a time when he trusted to himself."

"When he said, 'Though all men should deny thee, yet will not I.'"

"Yes; there was no 'Lord, thou knowest,' then. He fancied himself the very best of all. But this was over now. Jesus seems to try if he imagined his love greater than the other disciples. Look at the words, 'Lovest thou me more than these?' That is, 'More than Nathanael and James and John and Thomas love me.' Does Peter say anything to this?"

"No, teacher."

"No. 'I love thee' is all that he can say. 'Whether more or less than the other disciples, I cannot tell; but it is with my whole heart, as thou, Lord, knowest.' Then what did Jesus say?"

"Feed my lambs." "Feed my sheep."

"Who are the sheep of Christ?"

"People that love him."

"The young." "Little children."

"Yes, when they truly give their hearts to him. Often and often have you been told, dear children, how Jesus loves them. He proves his love here; and he shows his love for Peter too. I said just now his companions might have supposed he was not to be any longer—"

"An apostle—"

"On account of his sin. But here Christ gives him back his apostle's work. 'Take again,' he says, 'the charge of my people and my cause. Take it in the presence of these your companions. Go and preach to all the love that has so freely pardoned you. Be PETER once again.' More than this: he must not only work, but suffer as a follower of Christ. Emily read the eighteenth verse."

The verse is read.

"What did this signify?"

"The death by which he should glorify God."

"Do any of you know what kind of death this was that Jesus predicted?"

Eliza remembers to have read that Peter was crucified.

"Yes; and do you recollect in what manner? 'I am not worthy,' he said—'I, who once denied my Saviour—to die a death like his; let me, therefore, be fastened to the cross with my head downward.' In this manner he was put to death. Thus, thirty-four years after these words of Christ, did he 'stretch forth his hands' upon the cross 'to glorify God' by a martyr's death. But till then Jesus commands him—"

"Follow me."

"When this was said, Jesus very likely rose to go. Peter followed. Who besides?"

"John, the disciple whom Jesus loved."

"And Peter, full of love and joy himself, was anxious to know what would become of his fellow-disciple. But Jesus said—"

"If I will that he tarry till I come, what is that to thee?"

"What did this mean?"

After a pause, Susan replies, "It was nothing to Peter when John should die."

"Exactly so, my dear. Peter had his own work to do; John had his. And when John should die, or even whether he should die at all, Peter had no right to ask. Christ himself watches over all his faithful servants, all his dear children, and calls them to his presence above just when he sees fit.

'Very soon may some of us all this weight of glory
    know;
But some the hoary head may bear, and sorrow's
    wrinkled brow:
It can be little matter whiche'er the lot we win,
If Christ shall dwell on earth with us, or we in heaven
    with him.'

I should like to have talked more to you about the love of Jesus to Peter, but our time is gone. Think, my dear children, that Christ asks you the question, too, 'Lovest thou me?' Thou, Susan, Charlotte, Emily, Mary Jane! Each must answer for herself. Oh, recollect, a day of solemn judgment will come, when you will be miserable indeed if you love not Christ. But on that day your heaven will be begun if, amid its terrors, you can peacefully look to Him who sitteth upon the throne, and say, as Peter said by that sea-shore, 'Lord, thou knowest all things; thou knowest that I love thee.'"

X.

TENTH SABBATH.

THE selection of such a subject as that which had now occupied the class so long had been at the outset quite an experiment. It was undertaken not without a fear that the discussion would prove too complicated for minds so young. "Harmonies" of the Gospels are so various in their conclusions and often so uncertain in their reasonings that the attempt to present one of their stock subjects to the investigations of childhood could not but seem very doubtful. With what success the task was accomplished has been seen; for these conversations, as stated at the first, are not imaginary. The children, as successive recapitulations proved, had retained a clear and strong perception of the series of events which followed the resurrection of our Lord. They could, without hesitation, refer to the successive particulars, each in its place, whether in the Evangelists or the Epistle to the Corinthians; and the minuter shades and touches in the beautiful narrative, only to be discovered by an attentive eye, had grown quite familiar to them. All seemed sorry that the subject was so nearly closed.

After brief reference to the seven appearances * of Christ, down to that scene on the shore of Gennesaret, the scholars were asked whether they had busied themselves in searching out the rest.

A ready affirmative gives the reply, which three or four of the girls further confirm by turning quickly to Matt. xxviii. and 1 Cor. xv. It is pleasant too to see that Susan has

* 1, To the women. 2, To Mary Magdalene. 3, To Peter. 4, To the two disciples on the road to Emmaus. 5, To the apostles without Thomas. 6, To the whole eleven. 7, To the seven disciples by the Lake of Tiberias.

her book open at Acts i., a chapter to which no reference had in previous conversations been made.

"Where, then, was the next appearance?"

"Upon a mountain in Galilee."

"To how many disciples?"

"To the eleven."

"To no more?"

After a pause Mary Jane reads, "He was seen of above five hundred brethren at once," 1 Cor. xv. 6, but doubtfully.

"I think you are right, Mary Jane; and that the five hundred of whom Paul speaks were on that mountain with the eleven. But does Paul say so?"

"No, teacher."

"Does Matthew?"

After a little search, the negative is repeated.

"Well, then, we cannot be quite sure; but we can find out what is likely. Shut up Matthew now, and look only to Paul. There, that is right. Now see: '*Five hun-*

dred *disciples?'* Where must they have lived?"

No answer. The scholars seem unable to discern their teacher's drift.

"Where did *most* of Christ's disciples live?"

"In Jerusalem." "In Galilee."

"Right. Galilee and Jerusalem. In these two places he had more followers than anywhere else. So that we should look for the five hundred, certainly, in one of them. Now, were there so many as five hundred in Jerusalem?"

Another pause. Susan then exclaimed, in sudden discovery: "No, teacher; the number of the names together was about an hundred and twenty."

"Exactly, my dear; so that we may be almost certain that this meeting of five hundred could only have been in Galilee. But now look to Matthew again. How did the disciples there spoken of feel when they saw Jesus?"

"They worshiped him, but some doubted."

"Doubted! Do you think the eleven apostles could have doubted *now?*"

"No, teacher. They had seen Jesus so many times."

"Quite right, my child. They were surely convinced. Others must have been with them on the mountain who had not heard and seen what they had. These doubted, as the apostles themselves had done before. And what Paul says makes it likely that this was the time when the 'five hundred brethren' were assembled. It is not wonderful that in so great a company some should be slow to believe. But now tell me what Jesus said to them."

"All power is given unto me in heaven and earth. Go ye, therefore, and teach all nations, baptizing them," etc., Matt. xxiii. 18-20.

"To whom did he say this?"

"To the apostles," says Harriet. "No, to the five hundred brethren," rejoins Mary Jane.

"Certainly, my dear, to all who were assembled there.* They were not all ministers, but they all knew something of his love. So they were to tell of that love, and each do all the good he could. Christ says, even to every little child that knows and loves him, Try to teach others my will. Tell them of my grace. Do all you can to lead them to seek me as their Saviour. You cannot indeed be missionaries; you cannot preach, you cannot yet even teach in the Sunday-school (though one or two of you, I hope, will soon begin), but you can do some good if your heart is only full of the love of Christ and you are truly anxious to find out a way. For Jesus himself has promised to be with you and give you his help. Read his own words."

"Lo, I am with you alway, even to the end of the world."

"Yes, my children; and they are words for you and me, and all who serve him, as surely

---

* The charge had already been given to the apostles in private, Mark xvi. 15.

as if we had stood upon that mountain, and listened to them there. Christ is with us; and if we therefore try with all our hearts to do his will, we must succeed. But we must pass on to his last appearances."

"After that," reads Mary Jane, "he was seen of James," 1 Cor. xv. 7.

"Yes, my dear; but of this appearance we have no other account. Do you think there were any visits of Jesus to his disciples not mentioned at all?"

In a moment or two Susan replies, "I should think so, teacher, because it is said in Acts i. 3 that he was 'seen of them forty days.'"

"Exactly so. This visit to James, and a great many interviews with the other apostles, no doubt happened in this time. How was the time spent?"

"In speaking of the things pertaining to the kingdom of God."

"Did Jesus return from Galilee?"

"Yes, teacher," answers Charlotte, reading

Acts i. 4: "'And, being assembled together, with them, commanded them that they should not depart from Jerusalem.'"

"You think, my dear, this shows that they had all returned to Jerusalem again? Well, that you are right the following verses prove. But now we come to the last appearance of all."

"When he ascended up into heaven," observes Harriet.

"And where have we the account of this?"

"In Acts i.," says Susan. "In Luke xxiv.," adds Emily.

"Nowhere else?"

"Oh yes, in Mark xvi.," rejoins Mary Jane.

"Keep, then, the three places open, and let us compare them. Where did the ascension of Jesus take place?"

"At Bethany," replies Emily. "On the mount called Olivet," answers Susan.

"Can both be right?"

Two or three of the scholars, who have lately been to see a model of Jerusalem, instantly reply, "Bethany was on the mount of Olives, teacher—*on the other side*, at the foot."

"On the opposite side to Jerusalem, you mean, I suppose. I am glad, my dears, you remember our visit to the model so clearly. How far was this from Jerusalem?"

"A Sabbath day's journey," says Susan. "About fifteen furlongs," adds Mary Jane, remembering John xi. 18.

"Yes, the place, I suppose, was near, not in Bethany; about a mile and a half from Jerusalem, down on the other side of Mount Olivet. What are you whispering to your sister about, Charlotte?"

Charlotte blushes and is silent. Susan replies, smiling, "The gentleman at the model told us that the ascension of Christ was from the 'middle summit' of the Mount of Olives, teacher."

"He did, my dear, but you see he was

mistaken. Well, as they were walking out toward Bethany, what did they converse about by the way?"

"The disciples asked Jesus, 'Lord, wilt thou at this time restore again the kingdom to Israel?'"

"What kingdom did they mean?"

"The kingdom of heaven."

"Ah, but what did they understand the kingdom of heaven to be?"

"That Jesus was to be a great king and reign on earth," replies Mary Jane.

"Yes, and they had not got rid of this notion yet, although Jesus had so plainly told them he was going to depart. What did Christ say to them?"

"It is not for you to know the times and the seasons, which the Father has put in his own power."

"As much as to say, 'Do not question. Wait. A time is at hand in which you will know all that is needful for you.' What time did Jesus mean?"

"The day of Pentecost."

"And what made the day of Pentecost so wonderful?"

"The coming of the Holy Ghost."

"Why was the Holy Spirit sent?"

"To teach the apostles," replied Susan, "why Christ had suffered and risen again."

"Yes; when this 'promise of the Father' was fulfilled, they understood at once what the kingdom of Jesus was. They need 'ask no more questions' (John xvi. 1). All was clear, all was beautiful! But as yet they were in the dark. They were now near Bethany, where they had so often been together. Not far off, through the trees, appeared the white walls of Martha's house. The villagers passed to and fro, not thinking of the wondrous event that was about to happen in silence so near. The Saviour stops in his walk. His disciples gather round him. He changes his words of instruction for words of blessing. His hands are outstretched over them. Their hearts are strangely melted.

Surely his form is changing! Then suddenly he rises from the earth. A bright descending cloud comes over him, and he is gone! Another instant, and the sky is clear and blue again. Astonished, speechless, they gaze up into heaven, when, behold—"

"Two men stood by them in white apparel."

"Angels of God, the two who had watched the sepulchre—and told them—"

"This same Jesus, which is taken up from you into heaven, shall so come in like manner as ye have seen him go into heaven."

"What did the disciples then do?"

"They returned to Jerusalem."

"Wonderingly, thankfully, hopefully; to wait together and pray together, in their upper room, for the promise of the Father, the Comforter, the HOLY GHOST. And where was JESUS?"

Harriet reads, "He was received up into heaven, and sat on the right hand of God."

" For what purpose are we told he is there exalted ?"

" As a Prince and Saviour, to give repentance to Israel and remission of sins," answers Susan. Mary Jane replies, " To make intercession for us." Harriet, " To prepare a place for us."

"And for whom, my dear, is that place prepared ?"

" For those who believe in him—"

" Who trust in the merits of his death and pray to God for his sake to be merciful to them. 'For all such he died. He rose and stayed a while on earth, to show that God had accepted his sacrifice and given him all power. And then he went up to heaven, that there he might present to his Father our feeble prayers, and open to us his kingdom of everlasting glory. My dear children, do you trust him as your Saviour? Remember, as those angels said, he will come again. Every eye will see him as he appears in the clouds of heaven. If we turn away from him or reject him now, he will then cast us off for ever. But if we trust and serve him, that day will be a day of joy indeed, for he will acknowledge us as his own children. Death will have lost its sting. The victory of the grave will be over. For God will have given us the victory, through our Lord Jesus Christ. My heart's desire and earnest prayer is, that all of you, my beloved scholars, with your teacher, may gain that victory at last, and so be 'for ever with the Lord.'

"And now, Harriet, before we quite close, I think you can repeat a hymn which speaks of the Saviour's coming again in glory."

A bright smile comes over the dear child's countenance, which changes at once into an expression of thoughtful seriousness, as she rises and begins:

> "Up in heaven, up in heaven,
> In the bright place far away,
> He whom bad men crucified
> Sitteth at his Father's side
> Till the judgment day.

TENTH SABBATH.

"And he loveth little children,
    And he pleadeth for them there:
Asking the great God of heaven
That their sins may be forgiven,
    And he hears their prayer.

"Never more a helpless baby,
    Born in poverty and pain,
But with awful glory crowned,
With his angels standing round,
    He shall come again.

"Then all wicked souls shall tremble,
    And the ransomed shall rejoice;
Parents, children, every one,
Then shall stand before his throne,
    And shall hear his voice.

"And the good and faithful servants,
    Who their Master's work have done,
Shall appear at his right hand,
And inherit the fair land
    That his love hath won."

THE END.

www.ingramcontent.com/pod-product-compliance
Lightning Source LLC
Chambersburg PA
CBHW020254170426
43202CB00008B/363